About the author:

Tui Snider is a freelance writer, travel blogger, and photographer specializing in offbeat sites, overlooked history, cultural traditions, and quirky travel destinations.

Her articles and photos have appeared in BMIbaby, easyJet, Wizzit, Click, Ling, PlanetEye Traveler, iStopover, SkyEurope, and North Texas Farm and Ranch magazines, among others. She also wrote the shopping chapter for the "Time Out Naples: Capri, Sorrento, and the Amalfi Coast 2010" travel guidebook. This is her first book.

For a media kit, or to contact the author directly, visit:
TuiSnider.com

UNEXPECTED
T E X A S

Your Guide to Offbeat & Overlooked History, Day Trips, & Fun things to do near Dallas & Fort Worth

by Tui Snider

To Mom & Dad for igniting my wanderlust,
& to Larry for fanning its flame.

UNEXPECTED
TEXAS

Table of Contents

INTRODUCTION

First Impressions of Texas: Lather, Rinse, Repent!

The state of Texas and I got off on the wrong foot. It wasn't the stark prairielands that depressed me; it was the human side of the landscape. On that first drive home from DFW Airport in the fall of 2009, the endless procession of strip malls, donut shops, "breastaurants" (a la Hooters), and churches lining the highway gave me the impression that all Texans did was eat junk food, leer at women, then repent on Sunday.

I must also confess to a hefty chunk of Yankee prejudice. Part of me thought I had Texas figured out, you know: big hair and BBQ, pick-up trucks and country music. Was I ever wrong! Sure, Texas is all those things, but what I did not realize then, and what this book intends to show, is that Texas is much more than all the news headlines and clichés would suggest.

Unexpected Texas

Shortly after my move, an online travel magazine recruited me to write about the Dallas - Fort Worth region. They needed three articles a week about fun things to see and do in north Texas. I immediately said yes, although at that point I had no idea what to see and do in Texas. It certainly made a great excuse to visit the library and bookstore.

After plowing through a pile of travel guides, almanacs, and history books, my perception of Texas began to change. As if I had misjudged an acquaintance, I realized that Texas has great stories to tell, but only if you ask the right questions. My earlier assumptions, based on the veneer of Texas, had blinded me to its depth. And while I wasn't sure what to do with it, I began amassing quirky history and lore about this fascinating state. You hold the result in your hands.

Although this book is chock full of quirky goodness, I am still learning about Texas and finding more and more offbeat and overlooked legends and sites to research and explore. I could easily write a sequel, and if you know of something wonderful that I have missed, please send me an email at TuiSnider@gmail.com with the subject "Unexpected

Texas." I will do my best to include it in future travel articles, blog posts, and guides.

In the meantime, let me briefly explain how this book is organized. Part One includes unexpected tidbits of Texas culture that apply statewide. These are things that intrigued me as a newcomer, and include topics that even some native Texans I know were surprised to learn.

In Part Two, I take you around north Texas, sharing offbeat and overlooked travel tips for places within a day's drive of Dallas and Fort Worth. Some of the quirkier chapters include details on how to visit the:

- Gravesite of an alleged space alien.
- Courthouse displaying an embalmed lizard in a velvet-lined casket.
- Statue of Jesus wearing cowboy boots.
- Museum commemorating the lynching of Santa Claus.
- Life-sized wax replica of Da Vinci's Last Supper.
- Building made entirely of salt.
- 65-foot-tall Eiffel Tower replica.
- Petrified wood cafe.
- World's smallest skyscraper.
- Only Michelangelo painting in America.

You can't make this stuff up. Actually you *can*, but here in Texas, you don't have to!

Website and Address Only

As someone who owns a lot of travel guides, I've learned that phone numbers, hours of operation, and admission prices quickly go out of date. Had I published this 10 years ago I would have included all that information, along with a reminder to double check such details before your outings. Due to the availability of the Internet these days, I have chosen to include only the address and website for each attraction in this guide – with a few exceptions.

Some offbeat sites are challenging to find, so in those cases I've added detailed written instructions along with the address. I should also add that while I sometimes received free admission and/or other discounts, the opinions expressed in this book are wholly my own.

Who is this book for?

This book is for Texans and non-Texans alike. Even if you never visit the Lone Star State, I hope you enjoy the history and trivia included here, and that it enlarges your idea of what Texas is all about.

Even Home is a Travel Destination

My travel philosophy boils down to a simple phrase: Even home is a travel destination. The world is only boring if you take everyone else's word for it. Offbeat and overlooked treasures exist everywhere, but you must actively seek them out. So whether you are in Texas or your own backyard, start exploring your hometown. You may be surprised by what you find.

PART ONE

Quirky, Offbeat & Overlooked Culture

Lady Bird's Bill

Each year, spring slams into Texas with all the subtlety of a meteor, leaving bright swathes of red, blue, and yellow wildflowers in its wake. On sunny days, it's common to see groups of people dressed in their Sunday best, posing for family photos in fields of bluebonnets by the roadway. While those who live elsewhere may not know their state's flower, it's a rare Texan who does not know that the bluebonnet is our official blossom.

Lady Bird Johnson's motto, "where flowers bloom, so does hope," is very apparent in Texas, and we have her to thank for this annual roadside display. The Highway Beautification Act of 1965 was even nicknamed "Lady Bird's Bill." At the time this was a snarky jab at her influence over the president, but it has since morphed into respect for the First Lady's appreciation of nature.

Will the Real Bluebonnet Please Stand Up?

Some confusion arises over which exact flower is the official Texan bluebonnet. Should you, when pressed for particulars, say *Lupinus subcarnosus*, or should you go with the more regional sounding *Lupinus texensis*? As it turns out, the Texas legislature declared five different members of the lupine family to be its official state flower. How's that for diplomacy?

Sadly, Texans are seeing fewer of their beloved bluebonnets each spring because an invasive weed, called *Rapistrum rugosum*, is sweeping across the state. This pretty yellow flower, known informally as Bastard Cabbage, germinates early, then chokes out other flowers such as Indian Paintbrush and bluebonnets.

Quince Celebrations

Besides colorful blossoms, you often see teenage girls in fancy ball gowns strolling through local parks here in Texas. These young women are accompanied by friends and family, also in formal attire, and there's usually a professional photographer in tow. While in some cases you are witnessing an outdoor wedding, most of the time this festive group is part of a Quince celebration.

A Quince celebration is a coming-of-age party for a 15-year-old girl. *Quince* means, "15" in Spanish, which is why the debutante is referred to as a Quinceañera. People often assume the tradition came from Spain, but its roots can be traced back to ancient Aztecan puberty rites. Like anything that's been around for centuries, the practice has changed over time. These days, Quince celebrations are primarily practiced by Hispanic Catholics, and is both a social as well as religious event.

Traditionally, a Quinceañera will have 14 *damas* (female attendants, rather like bridesmaids) and 14 *chambelanes* (male escorts), and a "man of honor" to accompany her. The celebration begins at a Catholic church with a special mass for the Quinceañera. Afterwards, the girl and her family head to a park for photos, and either have a picnic there, or meet elsewhere for a reception. Other traditional elements may include a bouquet for the Quinceañera to symbolize her new life, as well as a ring, a religious medal, and/or a tiara.

Often included in a Quince ritual is the *última muñeca*, or, "last doll." After her parents give the Quinceañera her *última muñeca*, she then passes the toy along to a younger sister or cousin to symbolize that as she comes of age, she leaves behind childish things and moves into adulthood. Like a wedding, how traditional, fancy and/or formal the event becomes is a choice the family makes.

What the heck is Juneteenth?

In this era of cell phones and social networking, it's easy to forget that news did not always travel so fast. Case in point: although Abraham Lincoln's Emancipation Proclamation took effect in 1863, Texan slaves did not learn of their freedom until more than 2 years later.

Juneteenth is the annual celebration of the day Texas finally got it straight. Union General Gordon Granger, backed by federal troops, took possession of Texas on June 18, 1865. On June 19th, 1865 General Granger gave a public reading of the Emancipation Proclamation from a balcony in Galveston. Ever since, both June 18 and 19 have been dates chosen to celebrate these historic events.

Juneteenth has been officially recognized as a holiday in the state of Texas since 1980. Even though banks and state offices remain open, some Texans take time off, while others still wonder "What the heck is Juneteenth?"

Danke schoen, y'all!

When people think of European immigrants coming to the USA, they often focus on New York's Ellis Island and forget that the port of Galveston also brought many newcomers to our country. Starting in the 1830's, tens of thousands of Germans entered the United States via Texas.

Although their cultural influence extends across the state, most of these Germans settled in the Hill Country, creating towns such as Fredricksburg, Boerne (pronounced, "bernie") and New Braunfels. While the German flag never flew over Texas, its language and food have deeply woven into the cultural fabric. Not only can you find German bakeries, delis, and restaurants throughout the state, but Texas even has its own German dialect.

German natives can understand the version spoken in Texas, but it comes with some unique features. Tex-German is more similar to 19th century German than what's spoken today. It's like a linguistic time capsule, studded with old-fashioned sentence structure and words that settlers made up along the way such as, "der Cowboy," "der Hamburger," and even, "die Office."

Not all of their linguistic additions are English words with, "der," and, "die," stuck in front of them. The Tex-German word for skunk, for instance, is *stinkkatze*, which literally means, "stinky cat." Meanwhile, in Germany, the word *skunktier* is used. Also, while the Tex-German word for a piano is *piano*, in Germany, they use *klavier*. Nor is there one concrete version of this Tex-German dialect; it varies widely from place to place, even family to family, in part because settlers came from different regions of Germany, and also as a result of the geographical distance of all these German-speaking towns from one another.

In the United States, most immigrant dialects disappear after two generations, so it's impressive that the Texas German dialect has endured in some families for up to five generations. In the 1940's, as many as 159,000 Texas residents spoke German as their first language. Even so, Texas German is dying out. Experts predict it will be completely gone by 2050.

Its decline began when anti-German sentiments flared up during World War I and World War II. Laws were passed mandating that English be spoken in churches and schools. At the height of this xenophobia, simply speaking German became a misdemeanor in places such as Travis County, and a Lutheran pastor in Corpus Christi was flogged for continuing his sermons in German. During WWII some American Germans were even sent to internment camps.

As a result, people began to fear speaking Texas German in public and quit passing it down to their children as frequently as they had in the past. Of the roughly 8,000 remaining native speakers of Texas German, in 2013 the youngest are in their 60's, so it's only a matter of time before the language dies out completely.

Thankfully, a German-born linguist named Hans Boas created the Texas German Dialect Archive project. Boas and his team members are busy recording, transcribing and translating the various types of German spoken throughout Texas while they still can. (For more information, check out the TGDP: Texas German Dialect Project website at: tgdp.org)

The Six Flags of Texas

Technically, Flag Day is June 14th, but it's easy to get the impression that Flag Day is every day here in the state of Texas. The Dallas - Fort Worth Metroplex is breezy, and all this wind power makes it easy to express your loyalty to state and country with proudly waving flags. Since moving here, locals often tell me that Texas is the only state in the USA allowed to fly its flag at the same height as the US flag. This, it turns out, is an urban legend, a rather believable one, I must say, but it's simply not true.

While Six Flags Over Texas is the name of a popular amusement park, it is also true that six different flags have flown over the state of Texas throughout the course of its history. Every Texan learned exactly which flags these were in school, but in case you are wondering, here they are:

Spain (1519-1685; 1690-1821)

France (1685-1690)

Mexico (1821-1836)

Republic of Texas (1836-1845)

US Confederacy (1861-1865)

US Flag (1845-1861; 1865-present)

I even came up with a silly mnemonic device to help you remember this info. All you need to do is mentally envision a pile of flags. That image helps you remember the phrase: state flags might really crumple up. The first letter of each word in the phrase matches the first letter of each flag that flew over Texas. Easy, huh?

PART TWO

Quirky, Offbeat & Overlooked Sites

ANTIQUE ALLEY TEXAS

Antique Alley Texas

Since 1999, several north Texas towns have joined forces to create a huge sale. Called Antique Alley Texas, this twice-yearly event stretches over 25 miles and runs through the little towns of Cleburne and Sand Flat all the way to Maypearl and Grandview.

The drive alone is worth the effort, since much of the journey takes you through tree-lined back roads and lush countryside. There may be no hint of Antique Alley Texas for a few miles, but just when you think you are lost, you will suddenly discover an oak grove full of antiques, a grassy lot jammed with food trucks, a roadside produce stand, or a simple knick-knack sale in someone's front yard.

Items for sale vary greatly in quality and price since Antique Alley Texas vendors range from professional artists and antique dealers to amateur crafters, as well as folks simply trying to do some spring cleaning.

Whatever the weather, Antique Alley Texas is held on the third Friday, Saturday, and Sunday of each April and September from 9:00 a.m. until 6:00 p.m. There's no telling what you will find. On my first jaunt, I enjoyed homemade ice cream at a roadside farm, sampled BBQ pork from a smoker on the back of a mammoth-sized pick-up truck, and had an amusing conversation with an elderly woman who was selling off her ex-husband's vintage *Playboy* magazine collection.

To get a conversation going in Cleburne, ask anyone you meet to explain Wampus Cats. While I got definitions from several locals, I'm still not clear on the matter. Nor could anyone in Grandview tell me why the zebra is their town mascot, although it certainly lends itself to graphically interesting signage and an eye-catching black and white striped water tower.

Plan your trip to Antique Alley Texas
Website: antiquealleytexas.com

ARCHER CITY

Overview of Archer City

Like many towns, Archer City bills itself as a friendly place on its official city website, and while I dismissed this as typical promotional hype, it turned out to be true – at least for me. As my husband and I strolled the perimeter of the stone courthouse in 110 degree weather, a man in a pick-up truck pulled over, rolled down his window, and asked, "Where y'all visiting from?"

The man laughed when he realized we only live a few hours away, saying, "Folks come from all over. Just last week, I met a couple from Holland." After pointing us towards a good place (as well as the only place) open for lunch, he added, "Have you found the bookstore yet?"

He was referring, of course, to that mecca for independent bookstore lovers, Booked Up, the legendary shop owned by Archer City's most famous native son, Larry McMurtry. You see, it's not the snazzy stone courthouse, the fact that it's the county seat, its distinction for being the

"Short Grass Ranching Capital of the United States," or even that Angela Kinsey (who portrays Angela Martin in "The Office") grew up here that attracts visitors to Archer City, Texas. The real draw here is books, and lots of them.

Booked Up

In 1988, Pulitzer Prize winning author Larry McMurtry returned to his hometown of Archer City, Texas with the dream of transforming it into a book-themed town. He even took out ads in literary magazines proclaiming, "Miraculous birth! Visit the newly born book town of Archer City, Texas, and help the endless migration of good books continue."

For those who can't quite place the name, Larry McMurtry has written dozens of novels, several of which have been turned into movies, including the Oscar-winning "Terms of Endearment" and "Brokeback Mountain."

Even if his name is not familiar, you may have heard of his book "Lonesome Dove" which was also a hit TV miniseries back in 1989. If Texas ever implements a citizenship test, it will certainly have a section dedicated to McMurty and "Lonesome Dove."

While "Texasville" and "The Last Picture Show" (more movies based on McMurtry novels) were filmed on the streets of Archer City, McMurtry's "book town" never quite came to fruition. Booked Up spread through several city blocks, but the rest of the town couldn't keep up. Over the past 30 years, other bookstores and book-themed bed and breakfast inns came along, but failed to thrive. In August 2012, worried that Booked Up might burden his heirs, McMurtry downsized his stock from some 450,000 books to a more manageable - but still huge - stock of around 200,000.

I visited Booked Up after this auction and still managed to get lost for several hours in the stacks. When you first walk into Building 1 (there are 4 all together) it feels like you've stepped into a farm house owned by a rancher who likes to read. The décor is homey, with well-worn furniture, mounted deer heads, and knick-knacks. I found several interesting books in this first room, but they were pricey; we're talking $200 and up. Luckily, other rooms had books in my price range and I came home with a couple of treasures.

Despite the massive downsizing, Booked Up's stock still fills an entire city block, and you can feel that it is a labor of love. Homemade signs throughout the labyrinthine shop are part of the fun. Most are collages made from old magazines and say things like, "If you are unable to locate an employee in this building, please feel free to wander about yelling 'yoo-hoo' and peering into storage rooms until completely frustrated. Then proceed to Building One where you will find patronizing employees busy at work or sitting around drinking coffee, laughing at you. Thank you."

In 2011, the long-divorced McMurtry got re-married. His new spouse is Norma Faye Kesey (widow of the author, Ken Kesey.) The newlyweds live down the street from Booked Up, so you never know when they might pop into the store.

Plan your trip to Booked Up
Website: bookedupac.com
Address: 216 S Center St, Archer City, TX 76351

The Royal Theater

With its beautiful retro style marquee, Archer City's Royal Theater makes a nice photo op as you walk around the town square. The venue features prominently in the Oscar-winning movie "The Last Picture Show" and while it no longer shows movies, it is home to various live performances including Texas opry, plays, and musical variety shows. The Royal Theater is also available to rent for private functions such as meetings and parties.

Plan your trip to The Royal Theater
Website: royaltheater.org
Address: 113 E Main St, Archer City, TX 76351

ATHENS

Overview of Athens

Athens, Texas is a town where travel books and online research led me on one wild goose chase after another. Despite websites and guidebooks touting Athens as both the "Home of the Hamburger" and the "Black-Eyed Pea Capitol of the World," I found little to sustain either claim as of 2013.

First off, the city no longer hosts its annual Black-Eyed Pea Festival, and if this little burg truly did invent the hamburger, none of the local eateries made such a boast. I think there's more evidence to sustain Kim Jong Il's claim to inventing the hamburger than anything I could find in Athens. Despite these false leads, I discovered a couple of offbeat and overlooked treasures in the town: an aquarium where you can fish, and a historic graveyard with beautiful marble monuments.

Texas Freshwater Fisheries Center

Have you ever been to a zoo where you could hunt? Me, neither! I do, however, know of an aquarium where you can fish: The Texas Freshwater Fisheries Center (TFFC) in Athens, Texas.

The Texas Freshwater Fisheries Center is a full production freshwater fish hatchery dedicated to the preservation of Texas wetlands. If you've ever been curious about the ecology of freshwater lakes you can see it up close and personal at this public facility. The TFFC maintains 300,000 gallons of freshwater fish exhibits, featuring catfish, gar, bass, and more. I especially enjoyed the alligator exhibit and the freshwater stream section.

Interactive Dive Show and Tram Tour

I suggest timing your visit so that you can see the freshwater dive show. There's a pre-show movie which gives an overview of all the projects in which the TFFC is involved. After that, a suited diver jumps into the tank, feeds several species of fish, tells you about their life cycles, and answers questions from audience members.

Immediately after the dive show, there's a free tram tour of the freshwater fish production facility. This is definitely worth it, and gives you another chance to ask questions. The staff and volunteers are friendly and enthusiastic.

If you're up to it, instead of riding the tram back to the main facility, walk back along the gorgeous wetland trail. It's paved, so it's easily maneuverable for strollers and wheelchairs. The trail is like an outdoor museum offering educational exhibits along the way. You can press buttons at a little gazebo to hear bird calls, for instance, or peek into a glass-covered honeybee hive as you stroll.

If you get a hankering to fish, the TFFC staff will let you borrow a rod, reel, and bait. They will even give you a free fishing lesson. You can then mosey out to the shaded fish ponds and give it a try. Who knows? You may wind up having fish for dinner.

Plan your trip to the Texas Freshwater Fisheries
Website: tpwd.state.tx.us/spdest/visitorcenters/tffc
Address: 5550 F.M. 2495, Athens, Texas 75752

Athens City Cemetery

Athens City Cemetery is a beautifully wooded graveyard, with several well-crafted headstones and historical markers. As someone who frequently haunts historic cemeteries, I must say that this is one of the prettiest I have found.

Athens City Cemetery is also the final resting place for some moderately famous folks. Here are a few headstones to keep your eyes out for:

Alton Delmore (1908 – 1964) and his brother Rabon Delmore (1916 – 1952) a bluegrass duo known for tunes such as "The Frozen Girl," "See that Coon in the Hickory Tree," and "Don't You See That Train?" (None of which I've ever heard of, but the titles are intriguing.)

Lionel Alton Delmore (1940 – 2002) This is the aforementioned Alton Delmore's son. He is known for the tunes "Beautiful Brown Eyes" and "Midnight Special" (both of which I've heard of.)

For any sports buffs who may be reading this, Athens Cemetery also includes the grave of the Major League Baseball outfielder Ray Pepper (1905 – 1996) who played for the St. Louis Cardinals and St. Louis Browns.

The most opulent headstones at Athens City Cemetery belong to the Wofford family. Their memorials feature beautifully carved angels and high quality marble. A more recent headstone features an etching of a longhorn cow standing in a field of bluebonnets. You can't get much more Texan than that!

Plan your trip to Athens City Cemetery
Address: 400 Prairieville St, Athens, Texas 75752

AURORA

Overview of Aurora, Texas

With over 1800 graves, Aurora Cemetery currently claims more inhabitants than the little town itself, with its population of 376. In the late 1800's, however, Aurora was poised for the big time. It boasted nearly 3000 residents, making it one of the largest cities in Wise County. Sadly, a spotted fever epidemic killed hundreds of residents, the cotton crop failed, and the railroad decided to pass by the town.

When you visit Aurora, Texas do not expect anything fancy. There's no courthouse, no historic town square, no central shopping area at all. There's so little to this town that it's nearly impossible to tell you are even there. So why visit Aurora, Texas? Why, to see the gravesite for an alleged space alien, of course!

Aurora Cemetery

Aurora Cemetery was established in 1861. Like many older graveyards, it has a Texas State Historical Marker. While pioneers, cattlemen, farmers, and soldiers often figure prominently on such signs, what makes this historical marker unusual is that it mentions a spaceship crash in 1897.

You've probably heard of the Roswell Incident, an alleged spaceship crash in the desert of New Mexico in 1947. While the Roswell Incident is arguably the most well-known case in UFO history, here in north Texas there exists an alleged extraterrestrial wreck (complete with an alien body) which took place 50 years earlier.

A spaceship crash in north Texas?

As the story goes, in the early morning hours of April 17, 1897 a mysterious craft crash-landed in the north Texas town of Aurora. According to a newspaper article which appeared in the April 19 edition of the *Dallas News*, a cigar-shaped airship ran into a windmill, spread debris across several acres and – strangest of all – a small humanoid body was discovered in the wreck. According to the reporter, although the petite alien was "not an inhabitant of this world," his or her body was buried in the local cemetery. (If you want to read the entire original article as published in the

Dallas News, it has been scanned and uploaded to several websites, including Wikipedia.)

What with epidemics, crop failure and being slighted by the railroad, the townsfolk of Aurora paid little attention to the odd incident. Given the mindset of the era and the challenges they faced, it's not surprising that instead of studying the alien's body for science, the locals buried the creature and moved on with their lives. No reports exist regarding the actual funeral ceremony, although a headstone was placed at the gravesite. According to photos and verbal accounts, this first headstone depicted a crudely carved cigar-shaped object with portholes in the side.

In any case, the weird incident faded into the background as the once-booming town of Aurora withered into near oblivion. Then, in 1973 a United Press International blurb mentioned the alleged spaceship crash reported in north Texas.

This little article created so much interest in the old story that local police had to guard the alien grave day and night to keep trespassers from digging it up. Sadly, the night they quit this vigil someone stole the original headstone for the space creature. There was even a push to officially exhume the alien's body, but the cemetery association declined.

Of course, there is also the strong possibility that the whole thing is a hoax.

Here's what debunkers say:

1. There was no windmill on Judge Proctor's land.

2. There is no well.

3. There is nothing buried beneath the gravesite.

4. There is no mysterious metal near the crash site.

5. The reporter made the story up hoping to make the town a tourist attraction.

Here's what believers say:

1. The History Channel found evidence of a windmill on Judge Proctor's land.

2. They found a well at this site, too. The well was capped in the 1950's because the owner thought it was contaminated by the alien debris. The History Channel convinced the current owner to let them uncap it and test the water.

3. Melted metal has been found in the alleged crash site area. This metal is not some unearthly element. It's aluminum. While aluminum seems commonplace to us now, it was actually quite rare in the late 1800's.

4. The History Channel also found, via ground-penetrating radar, a casket-shaped item in the ground exactly where the alien is allegedly buried. (While the original tombstone was stolen in 1973, a new grave marker, which I've seen, was added by the local townspeople back in 2000. Unfortunately, as of this writing the alien's headstone has been stolen once again.)

5. The 1947 Roswell Incident crash debris was taken to Fort Worth, Texas which is only 30 minutes away from Aurora.

6. The town of Aurora is set up like a military base. (I'm not sure what they mean by this, since as I mentioned earlier the town of Aurora is barely there. I did notice a street called, "Base," but beyond that, I don't understand this claim.)

While I don't think there is conclusive proof that an alien crashed to earth here in north Texas, I do think something unusual happened in Aurora back in April of 1897. Sadly, it is such a cold case that we may never know the truth.

I definitely wish the Aurora Cemetery would let a respected investigation group exhume the alien's coffin and see what is really in there. Maybe there's a note saying that the whole thing is a prank. The cemetery board very nearly exhumed the body back in 1973. What are they afraid of?

There was a rash of, "mysterious cigar-shaped airship," sightings all across the US, but especially in Texas, in 1896 and 1897. Some of the accounts are downright ridiculous. In one I came across, the aliens reportedly sang religious hymns and had a barbecue.

Perhaps what makes the Aurora incident so enduring is that – even if it is just a tall Texan tale – its details dance along the edge of possibility without plunging overboard and landing in the utterly implausible. This is good advice for storytellers (and other professional liars) everywhere. Then again, to paraphrase Freud, "Sometimes a cigar-shaped object is just a cigar-shaped object."

Unique Headstones: These Boots Were Made for Walker

Even without the bizarre UFO incident, if you enjoy historic cemeteries, the Aurora Cemetery is very pretty and is full of bluebonnets in the springtime. It also has some of the most unique headstones I have seen.

As you face the main gate, on the left side of the entryway there are several graves for members of the Walker family featuring carved cowboy boots, riding boots and even a pair of black pumps. I don't yet know the story behind these shoe-themed headstones, but if you ever visit this cemetery they are worth a gander.

Plan your trip to Aurora Cemetery

Aurora Cemetery address: There is no official street address for Aurora Cemetery, but it's not hard to find. If you have a GPS, set it for: Cemetery Rd, Aurora, TX 76078. If not, head towards Rhome, Texas on US 81/287. Exit onto Highway 114, drive roughly 1.5 miles then turn onto Cemetery Road. The cemetery will be on your left hand side.

How to find the Space Alien Gravesite: To find the alien gravesite, turn right as you enter the Aurora Cemetery gates. It's pretty easy to find if you look in the older section of the graveyard. There aren't any graves near it. Perhaps people were creeped out at the idea of being buried near the creature, or – since the alien didn't have any family members – there was simply no one to put beside him or her. As mentioned earlier, as of this writing the headstone was stolen. There is usually some sort of marker there, though. Last time I went, there were plastic flowers and a handful of pennies marking the area where the headstone had been.

AZLE

Overview of Azle, Texas

With its proximity to Fort Worth, the little town of Azle, Texas offers small town living within easy reach of the big city. There's no town square, but there are some interesting things to see and do here.

Wild West Toys and the Music Centre

If you enjoy retro collectibles, Wild West Toys will knock your socks off. The shop is stocked with vintage playthings from the 1950's and 60's, as well as specialty sodas (sarsaparilla and the like), candies, turquoise jewelry, western-themed dishes, housewares, and play clothes for kids. Wild West Toys is also the only place in the USA to manufacture metal cap guns. They must be top notch, too, because even Chuck Norris owns a pair (and there are photos on the shop's website to prove it.)

This fun little store is owned by Bob Terry and his wife, Johnny. Despite being responsible business owners with kids of their own, the duo are clearly in touch with their inner children. Check out their YouTube channel, where they post homemade westerns following the adventures of "the cap gun kid," and other playful western-themed videos.

Plan your trip to Wild West Toys
Website: wildwesttoys.com
Address: 106 West Main Street, Azle, Texas 76020

Azle Antique Mall

Azle is also home to a 16,000 square foot antique mall. Although crammed to the gills, the shop is clean and the inventory is well-organized. Here you can find all sorts of collectibles, ceramics, glassware, jewelry, coins, housewares, quilts, and more.

Azle Antique Mall is owned by Phil and Heather Coomer. Phil writes novels, one of which was recently made into a movie called "A Bird of the Air." You can find this video as well as Mr. Coomer's novels for sale alongside all the antiques. (I've since read the book and seen the movie and enjoyed them both.)

Plan your trip to the Azle Antique Mall
Website: burlesonantiquemall.com
Address: 1951 Northwest Pkwy, Azle, TX 76020

Azle Opry

Marshall Holmes founded the Azle Opry back in 1963. It all started when Holmes and his friends would meet for jam sessions behind the laundry he owned. Over time, Holmes removed all the washers and dryers and started calling the place the Azle Opry instead of the Coin-O-Mat. Although Mr. Holmes passed away in 2013 at the age of 86, his weekly live music show is still going strong.

Every Friday night at 7:00 p.m. a local band kicks off the evening. After a while, singers and musicians are invited to join them on stage for a song or two. While the Azle Opry has plenty of regulars, it's a friendly crowd and newcomers are welcome. The music leans towards country, but other genres are encouraged, too.

Unlike most places in Texas, the Azle Opry has been a non-smoking establishment for many years. Drinking and swearing are also forbidden. Admission is free, although the Azle Opry relies on donations received when they pass the hat.

Plan your trip to the Azle Opry
Address: 124 S. Stewart, Azle, Texas 76020

Smoke Rise Farm

Texas is full of historic graveyards and I love exploring them. I rarely visit modern cemeteries, unless there is someone famous buried there or a particularly unique headstone to check out. For the most part, newer graveyards lack the history, the beautiful old trees, and the finely crafted headstones and monuments of the older ones.

Even so, Azle has an interesting cemetery that has only been around since 1982. It's a pet cemetery, and I'd never seen an official one before, so I wasn't sure what to expect. For one thing, the phrase, "pet cemetery," brings Stephen King's creepy novel to mind. For another, Azle is such a small town that I worried its pet cemetery would be little more than someone's backyard dotted with St. Francis of Assisi statues.

My suspicions deepened as the GPS announced, "You have reached your destination," since at that moment, we were surrounded by homes in a modest neighborhood. We decided to keep driving, however, and soon spotted the graveyard on our left.

Smoke Rise Farm Pet Cemetery is quite an operation. At 5 acres, it's much larger than I expected. Like any other cemetery, it's dotted with headstones and bouquets in a tranquil setting. The well-groomed grounds even feature a gazebo.

The main differences between Smoke Rise Farm and a cemetery for humans is the types of names you see on the headstones as well as the statuary. Where else are you going to see graves labeled: Doogie Bowser, Fifi La Fluff Nstuff or Puffy Buzzard? From what I could tell, the most popular pet name here in north Texas seems to be Muffin. As expected, there were plenty of St. Francis of Assisi statues, but I also saw statues of poodles, dachshunds, cats, ferrets and even a gorilla.

Another big difference between a pet cemetery and a human one is that the lifespans indicated on the graves is much shorter. The longest lifespan we saw at this pet cemetery was on the grave of a horse, which lived to a hearty 30 years of age.

Plan your trip to Smoke Rise Farm
Website: smokerisefarmpetcemetery.net
Address: 11330 Mountain View Dr, Azle, TX 76020

DALLAS

Overview of Dallas, Texas:

With a population pushing 1.3 million, Dallas is the ninth largest city in the USA, as well as the largest land-locked metropolis in the nation. While most major cities are situated on a navigable body of water, the main ports in Dallas are airports, not rivers or the sea. Speaking of airports, the Dallas - Fort Worth International Airport boasts the world's largest parking lot.

Unusual Trivia and Facts about Dallas:

One of the first things to pop into people's minds when they think of Dallas is the assassination of President John F. Kennedy. Plenty of books have been written about this tragic event, so I won't cover it here. Instead, let me present you with a list of ten offbeat and overlooked facts about Dallas, Texas:

1. The Dallas Arts District is the largest urban arts district in America, and on any given evening there are 110 or more live performances to choose from.

2. Dallas offers more restaurants and shopping centers per capita than any other major US city.

3. Fair Park in Dallas is the only pre-1950's world fair site in America still standing, and contains the biggest collection of Art Deco architecture in the nation.

4. The cornerstone of Dallas' Woodrow Wilson High School contains a piece of wedding cake from President Wilson's daughter, Jessie.

5. Two of PBS' most famous fictitious animals hail from Dallas: Barney the purple dinosaur and Wishbone the history-buff hound.

6. While many successful movies, including "RoboCop" and "Born on the Fourth of July," were filmed in Dallas, "Zyzzyx Road," starring Tom Sizemore and Katherine Heigl premiered here in 2006. Don't feel bad if you've never heard of it. "Zyzzyx Road's" main claim to fame is for being the lowest grossing film of all time. It only cleared $30 at the box office.

7. After being held at an internment camp near Dallas, at least one WWII German prisoner of war petitioned to become a permanent resident of the USA. (Come for the war, stay for the barbecue?)

8. Jack Kilby invented the microchip while working for Texas Instruments in Dallas.

9. The Dallas Public Library's permanent collection includes the First Folio of William Shakespeare's "Comedies, Histories & Tragedies" as well as one of the original copies of the United States Declaration of Independence.

10. KERA, a Dallas-based PBS station was the first television station to broadcast Monty Python's Flying Circus back in 1974.

Dallas Farmers Market

While Seattle's Pike Place Market is a staple in tourist guides for that region, the Dallas Farmers Market is often overlooked in similar guides for north Texas, which is why I include it in this one. Not only is it open seven days a week 362 days a year, but you better wear walking shoes because, in true Texan form, it is big.

If you enjoy locally-grown produce, look for the yellow "certified local" sign, which means that particular item was grown within a 150-mile radius of Dallas. Vendors supplement locally grown items with fresh out-of-state produce, as well.

Visiting the Dallas Farmers Market is one time that shopping hungry is advisable, because sellers are eager to offer samples. I tried several new things on my visit, including fruit from a prickly pear cactus. Shop early for the best selection, and shop late for the best deals. Most vendors take cash only, so don't bring big bills. I thought I was pretty clever for having my own shopping bag, until I saw a family pulling a Red Flyer wagon with an ice chest - now that was savvy. The market is packed on weekends, so if you have a lot of questions for vendors, go on a weekday, when it's not as crowded.

The indoor section of the Dallas Farmers Market is a good place to grab a bite to eat and to cool off, since it's air-conditioned. This is also where you find a variety of specialty food vendors: hormone free meats, organic tea and coffee, smoked sausage, Texas olive oil, and much, much, more.

The Dallas Farmers Market hosts special events throughout the year. The market also offers a meeting space with a demo kitchen and cooking classes. There is a large nursery adjacent to the market, as well as shops offering garden statuary and other supplies. Check out the official website for a list of what is currently in season, or simply head on down the Dallas Farmers Market and see what your local growers have brought to the city today.

Plan your trip to the Dallas Farmers Market
Address: 1010 S. Pearl Expressway, Dallas, TX
Website: dallasfarmersmarket.org

Old Red Museum

Since it's open 7 days a week and located smack in the heart of downtown Dallas, a trip to the Old Red Museum is the perfect reply to, "What shall we do next?" on a day of sightseeing in the Big D. Whether you are interested in politics, archeology, or those intriguing little details which made life so different in the past, it's got something to interest you. The museum chronicles regional history from ancient times right up to the present day, offering something for all age levels and attention spans. Visitors can learn about everything from the ancient mammoth to the notorious Bonnie and Clyde, through 41 touch screen monitors, four theaters, and five separate display rooms.

At first glance, it didn't seem like there was much to see, but once I sat at a touch screen monitor and got the scoop on Mary Kay, Southwest Airlines, 7 Eleven and other businesses born in the Big D, I was hooked. Those monitors and headsets convey a lot of information in an engaging way. Hearing firsthand accounts of the capture of Bonnie and Clyde from law enforcement agents and reporters while watching photos and film from that time is so much better than simply reading a plaque on the wall next to a static display.

I wasn't the only one who got sucked in. The group I was with quickly scattered, as we all found things of interest to learn about. In fact, we were all still exploring when the docent came through and rounded us up at closing time.

For those with internet access through their cell phones, the museum offers the Old Red Audio Tour. One of my friends tried this, putting his phone on speaker so we could all listen in. I didn't find out until later that you can press *0 during the audio tour to leave comments, which is a nice touch.

Chances are, if you have driven through downtown Dallas, you have noticed the Old Red Courthouse. With its turrets, gargoyles, archways, and beautiful red sandstone brickwork, it is an eye-catching building, and delightfully old-fashioned beside all the modern skyscrapers that flank it. Old Red is actually the sixth courthouse to be built in Courthouse Square, which is what John Neely Bryan labeled this area when he founded Dallas. How optimistic that after the first five burned down, the city chose to create such an impressive building in the same spot.

Before becoming a museum, Old Red served as a social hub for Dallas, hosting dances, funerals, auctions and other social gatherings in its elegant halls. Before moving to Pearl Street, the Dallas Farmers Market took place on the courthouse lawn. Even now, the top floor is still a rental facility for chic occasions. The day I was there, a steady stream of tuxedo-clad men were wandering about.

Plan your trip to the Old Red Museum
Website: oldred.org
Address: 100 S. Houston St. Dallas, TX 75202

Dallas World Aquarium

Don't let the name fool you, the Dallas World Aquarium is more than just a fun place to see exotic fish. I included it in this book because even locals seem to be under the false impression that due to the name it's "just another aquarium" when it also includes birds, jaguars, tropical plants, penguins, and more. Even the nondescript exterior of this former warehouse belies the lush interior inside. Before you even buy a ticket, you can enjoy a "Wilds of Borneo" display featuring animals from Indonesia which is visible from the outside of the building.

You then enter at the canopy level of a humid rainforest environment called the "Orinoco – Secrets of the River" display. Walkways let you meander through treetops, where several bird species fly through the branches – completely uncaged. Footpaths continue to the ground level and even below, where you can watch manatees, water fowl, and fish swim around a 40-foot waterfall. The plants are amazing, too. It's like walking through a huge South American terrarium.

My favorite part of the Dallas World Aquarium is a long acrylic viewing tunnel which allows you to watch sharks and rays cruise right over your head. It's a great photo op, but here's a tip: go during the weekday to avoid crowds in the view tunnel. It can get really stuffy in there.

While this is obviously good family fun, the Dallas World Aquarium is also a great place to take a date. There's so much to see; you can easily make a day of it. You don't even have to leave for lunch; the place has three restaurants, plus they serve beer, and ice cold margaritas. What's not to love?

Plan your trip to the Dallas World Aquarium
Website: dwazoo.com
Address: 1801 N Griffin St, Dallas, TX 75202

Kalachandji's Restaurant & Palace

As I mentioned earlier, Dallas has more restaurants per capita than any other major city in the US. That said, here in the land of Tex Mex, beef, and barbecue, vegetarian restaurants are not a common sight, which is why I'm including this wonderful eatery as an offbeat and overlooked place to eat.

On my first trip to Kalachandji's Restaurant and Palace in Dallas, Texas, I thought the GPS was confused as it steered us into a humble neighborhood with older houses and big trees. But then I saw it: In what must be a relief to limerick writers across the globe, there actually is a palace in Dallas.

Kalachandji's Restaurant and Palace in Dallas, Texas is located in a Hare Krishna temple, but don't let that scare you off. No one is out to push their religious beliefs on you. Every time I have eaten there, the wait staff is so pleasant and courteous that I'm tempted to find more places of worship at which to dine. Plus, I love sitting in their garden courtyard with its stained glass windows and gorgeous tree in the center.

Rock Stars and Rocking Reviews

On your way into the buffet line, take a look at all the framed press reviews on the wall. Several rock stars, such as Todd Rundgren, Peter Gabriel and Billy Corgin have autographed photos here, as well. A thank you letter from Annie Lennox reads in part: "You have created an oasis in this desert of slaughterhouses."

Kalachandji's Restaurant and Palace serves gourmet vegetarian cuisine following stringent guidelines, which they explain in detail on their official website. Not only is the cuisine meatless, but it also contains no eggs, onion, or garlic. For those who find restaurant dining a challenge due to allergies or other limitations, Kalachandji's is worth investigating.

That said, plenty of omnivores come to this restaurant as well. Why? Because meatless or no, the food is really good! Take me, for instance; I'm a self-described opportunivore, by which I mean if something looks good, I'll take a bite. At Kalachandji's, there is a lot that looks (and tastes) good.

Food here is served buffet style, and it's fine to return for seconds. I often take a tiny sample of several items, then return for a larger portion of ones I like. The menu changes daily, so if you want to know what's being served in advance, check out Kalachandji's Restaurant and Palace official website.

Cooking Classes

While you can find plenty of incense, jewelry, and other interesting items in the restaurant's little gift shop, there is no Kalachandji cookbook for sale. There is, however, an ongoing set of cooking classes. For details, check out their website.

Plan your trip to Kalachandji's
Website: kalachandjis.com
Address: 5430 Gurley Ave, Dallas, TX 75223

DECATUR

Wise County Courthouse

The Wise County Courthouse in the heart of Decatur's historic town square is a great place to start your visit to this adorable little town. If you've ever been to Waxahachie, Texas this building may seem like a petite version of that town's courthouse, and rightly so; both were designed by James Riely Gordon. (Yes, it's really spelled "Riely.")

Gordon's Romanesque Revival style building was completed in 1896 and features pink granite with terra cotta accents. There is more to Gordon's design than just good looks; the corner entrances actually keep air circulating and help cool the building. If you ask the County Auditor nicely, you may even be allowed to climb the stairway up to the tower, where you have sweeping views of the town and surrounding countryside.

Keep an eye out for plaques commemorating the Chisholm Trail, which is the route ranchers used to drive their cattle from their farms in Texas up to railheads in Kansas in the late 1800's. These days, Decatur has an annual

Chisholm Trail Steak Challenge at the local fair grounds each fall. The cook-off offers cash prizes for the best dishes, including $2500 for the best steak.

Famous Saying: Eighter From Decatur

If you like to gamble, you have probably heard the saying, "Eighter from Decatur, county seat of Wise." If you're not a gambler, you will definitely notice banners with "Eighter from Decatur" all over the city. Here's the story behind that famous saying: A fellow named Will Cooper, who held odd jobs around town, fell in love with a servant girl named Ada who lived in Decatur in the late 1800's. When playing craps, Mr. Cooper would chant, "Ada from Decatur, County Seat of Wise," and his catchy rhyme became popular in the area.

It probably would have ended there, but sometime around the year 1900, Will Cooper took a job cooking for a group of men traveling to Virginia to reenact the battle of Manassas. It was a long train ride, and along the way, the men often gambled. Mr. Cooper's catchy rhyme spread from there and along the way, "Ada" morphed into "Eighter." In 1949, Decatur mayor Sly Hardwick added "Eighter from Decatur" to the town's welcome signs and it's been part of the local identity ever since.

Decatur Glass

A variety of mom and pop shops surrounding the courthouse will keep you entertained for an afternoon. Keep an eye out for Decatur Glass in the antique stores. This hand-blown glass was produced in Decatur in the 1950's and 1960's at Tex Glass, Inc, a glass company started by husband and wife team, Bertha and Hermann Rosenzweig. Mr. Rosenzweig fled to the states after being persecuted by the Nazis. He eventually settled in Decatur and began producing his unique crinkle style glassware. It's now a collectible and can be found at some of the local antique stores surrounding the courthouse.

Plan your trip to Historic Downtown Decatur
Website: decaturmainstreet.com
Address: 101 N Trinity St #101, Decatur, TX 76234

Texas Tourist Camp

Other fun things to see in Decatur, Texas are its well-maintained petrified wood buildings. In 1927, E.F. Boydston bought a feed lot in Decatur, Texas and turned it into the Texas Tourist Camp. As grand as that sounds, at first it was merely a gas station with a few campsites beside it. Next came a restaurant, which started as the Texas Lunchroom, but soon became known as the Texas Cafe.

Petrified Wood Motel & Infamous Guests

In the 1930's, Mr. Boydston added several cabins with attached garages, thereby creating a rustic motel for tourists passing through town on the new highway. In 1935, he spruced things up by covering all the buildings in petrified wood. It's rumored that shortly before their bloody demise, the infamous gangster duo, Bonnie and Clyde stayed a night or two here.

Business boomed at the gas station, cabins, and restaurant until the 1960's, when the highway was diverted to the west side of town. With fewer people driving by, business withered away. The café went under in 1964, the cabins scraped by until 1970, and the gas station finally closed its doors in 1989.

It looked as though the petrified wood complex was going to go the way of the dinosaur, or at least fall to rack and ruin like so many places I see in north Texas.

A Petrified Wood Renaissance

Thankfully, one of E.F. Boydston's grandkids, Nancy Rosendahl and her husband Jim, stepped in to restore the petrified wood buildings in the 1990's.

These days, Jim uses the old gas station as an office, while the restaurant (now called the Whistle Stop Café) is a local hot spot. On the day I dined there, the food was good and the joint was jumping.

Please note: As a big fan of Fannie Flagg and her novel *Fried Green Tomatoes at the Whistle Stop Café*, I was excited to find an online menu for this venue featuring fried green tomatoes as a side dish. Sadly, that is an outdated menu from an earlier incarnation of the restaurant. As of this writing, the current Whistle Stop Café in Decatur does not have much of a web presence and seems to change its menu frequently.

Plan your trip to the Texas Tourist Camp
Address: 904 S Business 81/287 Decatur, 76234

DENTON

Overview of Denton

Denton is a thriving college town known for its lively music scene. Many well-known musicians have either lived or attended school in Denton. Sly Stone and Sarah Jaffe grew up in Denton, for example, while Roy Orbison, Michael Lee Aday (a.k.a. Meat Loaf), Don Henley, and Norah Jones all attended local universities. In addition, its University of North Texas was the first school to offer a degree in jazz studies.

Annual events that put this city on the map include the North Texas State Fair and Rodeo, and the Denton Arts and Jazz Festival, which attracts more than 300,000 music lovers to the city every year. Denton's music scene is regularly covered in *The Dallas Observer*, and has also been featured in *The New York Times*, *The Guardian*, and *Pop Matters*. In 2008, Denton's music scene was named best in the country by *Paste Magazine*.

With all that buzz, Denton seems poised to become the "Austin of the north" especially since 2009, when locals created North by 35, their version of Austin's famous springtime music festival, South by Southwest.

Denton County Courthouse-on-the-Square

Don't confuse Denton's new courthouse with its old one. There's no reason to visit Denton County Courts Building (the new one) unless you have business there. For a fun outing, head to the old one, known as Denton County Courthouse-on-the-Square. As the name implies, this building is on the city's town square and despite the city's current population of 113,383, the area is walkable, with a pleasant small town feel.

Built in 1896 using native Texas limestone, Denton's Courthouse-on-the-Square is a gorgeous Romanesque Revival style building that's listed on the National Register of Historic Places. The grand structure is flanked by locally owned eateries, shops, and cafes, some of which have been in business since the 1940's. The square is especially pretty during the annual Denton Holiday Lighting Festival in the fall, when all the trees and buildings are draped in white lights.

Plan your trip to Courthouse-on-the-Square
Address: 110 W. Hickory, Denton, TX 76201
Website: dentoncounty.com

Recycled Books

On my first trip to Denton, I made the mistake of visiting on a Sunday. Despite its size, downtown Denton is pretty dead on Sundays. Luckily, there was a fabulous indie bookstore open, a place called Recycled Books.

I love any bookstore, but funky, used bookstores are my favorites. The moment I stepped inside Recycled Books, I caught a whiff of used books, saw a huge room crammed with well-labeled sections and knew we had stumbled upon a gem.

At that point, I didn't realize that there was also a massive basement to explore, but I was still quite impressed. All in all, Recycled Books is 17,000 square feet of used book deliciousness. It more than made up for visiting Denton on a Sunday.

I even learned a new word while strolling through Recycled Books: Texana, which the staff informed me is a term used to describe all things Texan. In fact, Texana, Texiana, and Texicana can all be used, but Texana is the most popular word these days. The book you hold in your hand right now (or are reading on an e-reader) is an example of Texana.

Plan your trip to Recycled Books
Website: recycledbooks.com
Address: 200 N Locust St, Denton, TX 76201

Ghosts of Denton, Texas: Haunted History Tour

One hot summer night, my husband and I popped over to Denton, Texas to experience the Ghosts of Denton Haunted History Tour led by Shelly Tucker, a professional storyteller. I've known Shelly for a few years online, but this was our first meeting in person, so I was excited about that, too.

The Ghosts of Denton tours leave from Jupiter House, a coffee shop on the east side of the town square every Friday and Saturday night at 8:00 p.m. and last about 90 minutes. The night of our visit, the city was full of people strolling around, looking for fun on a warm summer night.

I recognized Shelley straight away; between her red hair and lively energy, she is hard to miss. (She is also hard to photograph; every picture I took of her was blurry because she was always moving!) Her tour that night was well-attended, with nearly two dozen folks, ranging in age from early teens to senior citizens.

Not Just for Ghost Hunters

What makes this haunted history tour fun is not so much the subject matter, but the fact that Shelly is a masterful storyteller. That lady can sure spin a yarn! Shelly could have led us on a tour of a thimble factory and we still would have clung to every word.

Even folks with no interest in the paranormal will find Shelly's tales interesting from a historical perspective. A few years ago, the National Endowment for the Arts (NEA) acknowledged her talents by naming her an "American Masterpiece."

It was clear that Shelly had much more material than we had time to hear. To my delight, after the group broke up, she took me and Larry for another spin around the square in order to share a story that was as she put it, "a little too racy for the young 'uns" on our tour.

Shelly is passionate about Denton's history and spends hours at the library digging up new material. She's now so well known as "the ghost lady" that people often pull her aside to confide their own ghost stories. As Shelly likes to say, "Sometimes folks come to Denton and never want to leave – ever!"

Plan your trip to Ghosts of Denton
Website: ghostsofdenton.com
Address: Jupiter House, 106 N Locust St, Denton, TX 76201

EASTLAND

Overview of Eastland, Texas

Despite the name, the city of Eastland is located in west Texas. (As an aside, the city of West, Texas is located in the south.) In the 1920's Eastland was a boomtown thanks to the oil industry. These days, it's a sleepy little town with a population hovering near 4,000. Don't let that fool you, however. This is one little town with a big past, a past including such things as a mural made from stamps to the lynching of Santa Claus. For starters, head to the town square where you will find the most famous resident of Eastland, Texas, a horny toad named Old Rip.

Horned Lizard Buried Alive

While the average horny toad has a lifespan of 5 to 10 years, there is an old wive's tale that – like Rip Van Winkle – they can live for 100 years in hibernation.

On July 29, 1897 a county clerk in Eastland, Texas named Ernest E. Wood decided to test this theory. On that day, a cornerstone containing a time capsule was cemented into the new Eastland County Courthouse. The time capsule included a Bible, coins, newspapers and – as a last minute addition by Mr. Wood – a live Texas horned lizard.

The reptile was his four-year-old son's pet, who the little guy named Blinky. I'm not sure how Mr. Wood's son, Will, reacted to his father's idea, but I know how I'd feel if my dad decided to bury one of my pets alive to, "test a theory."

Still Alive 31 Years Later

Thirty-one years later, that Eastland County Courthouse was demolished and a new one built. People remembered the Texas horned lizard that had been sealed in the cornerstone, and curiosity grew so strong that over 3,000 people arrived on February 18, 1928 to witness the cornerstone as it was unsealed.

Would the little critter be alive or dead? (I'm sure a bit of money exchanged hands that day; how could people resist placing a bet on something like that?)

Investigators Called In: It's No Hoax

To ensure no hanky-panky, the event was presided over by a judge and a Methodist pastor. Upon opening the cornerstone, a dusty horned lizard was found inside. Shortly afterwards, the creature began to wiggle and was deemed alive.

A biology team from Texan Christian University (TCU) examined the horned lizard and discovered that while it was healthy overall, it had a broken leg and worn-down horns, probably from trying to escape over the years. Blinky's eyes and mouth were sealed shut, as well, which is normal for a hibernating lizard at that time of year. (Incidentally, TCU's mascot is the Texas horned lizard, but they came up with that long before the whole Old Rip scenario. TCU did recently name a sculpture in Old Rip's honor.)

When some folks grumbled that the lizard's survival was a hoax (probably those who lost money on their bets!) a local businessman offered $1000 to anyone who could scare up a horny toad in Texas in February. Since horned lizards hibernate underground throughout the winter, no one was able to take up this offer. Other folks, including Will Wood, the boy – now a man – who had originally caught the lizard, attributed its survival to the Bible it was sealed up with rather than anything biological. This is Texas, after all.

Old Rip Goes Viral, Meets the President, Lives the Good Life

As news of the horned lizard's survival swept the nation, Blinky's publicists cleverly renamed him "Old Rip," as a nod to the Rip Van Winkle fairy tale.

What happened next, you ask? A national tour of the USA, of course! Old Rip was even given an audience with President Calvin Coolidge and written up in the pages of *Ripley's Believe it or Not!*

Keeping horned lizards as pets became a fad and a local Texas gas station handed out live horned lizards with every fill-up. Eastland County even tried to seal up another horned lizard in the cornerstone of the newest courthouse, but was dissuaded by the Fort Worth Humane Society at the last minute.

When not on tour, Old Rip lived with the Wood family in Eastland, Texas. Will Wood, who had originally caught the horned lizard as a toddler, now had children of his own, and they are the ones who took care of the famous lizard.

Sadly, Old Rip died from pneumonia on January 19, 1929, a mere 11 months after his initial release from the courthouse cornerstone. Will Wood had Old Rip preserved and obtained a tiny, velvet-lined coffin from The National Casket Company. After an open casket wake at a local funeral home, the lizard was exhibited at the town courthouse. Then, instead of being buried, Old Rip continued to travel the country as part of fairs and exhibits.

The legend of Old Rip became such a part of Eastland, Texas that it inspired several businesses including the Old Rip Cap Company, the Old Rip Café and Old Rip Soda. Even Warner Brothers took inspiration from the Old Rip tale when it created Michigan J. Frog, the character which symbolizes its TV network.

Gubernatorial Photo Op with Lizard Goes Awry

Eventually, Old Rip was returned to the Eastland Texas Courthouse where he can be viewed to this day. Even so, did returning home and being dead stop the adventures of this famous reptile? No way!

In 1962, gubernatorial candidate John Connally visited Eastland and wanted to pose with the famous lizard. Unfortunately, Mr. Connally accidentally broke a leg off of

Old Rip during the photo op, and the incident was kept hush-hush for many years.

Old Rip is Kidnapped – More than Once!

In 1964, Old Rip was kidnapped as a publicity stunt for the local Jaycees, which seems innocent enough. In 1973, however, a more serious lizard-napping caper ensued when Old Rip was snatched yet-again from the Eastland County Courthouse.

A ransom note soon followed, which along with the request for a small sum of money, claimed that Old Rip's survival for 31 years in the courthouse time capsule had been a hoax. The author of the note claimed to be one of the original conspirators and demanded that his or her co-conspirators should step forward. No one did.

Eventually, however, Old Rip's remains were recovered at the local fairgrounds. Ever since that incident, the town of Eastland, Texas has been a little more careful with the body of their most famous resident.

For the record: Horny toads are neither frogs nor toads. They are members of the lizard family, not amphibians. Still, the way their middle puffs out makes them look rather frog-like, and Texans often call them horny toads, which is why I use the terms interchangeably in this chapter.

For more on Old Rip, search YouTube for a 20-minute documentary called "Toadspotting."

Plan your trip to see Old Rip
Address: Eastland County Courthouse, 100 W Main St, Eastland, TX 76448

Eastland's Infamous Santa Claus Lynching

One of the biggest manhunts in Texas state history was for none other than Santa Claus. But before I go further, let me set the scene:

While "Wanted: Dead or Alive," is the phrase commonly associated with bounty posters, back in 1927, the Texas Bankers Association (TBA) did away with the, "or alive," clause and began offering a reward of $5000 for each dead bank robber that citizens or law enforcement could produce.

Dead Bank Robber Reward Program

Called the Dead Bank Robber Reward Program, this bounty was in response to a massive crime wave in the 1920's and 1930's. By the late 1920's, Texas was experiencing an average of three to four bank robberies every single day!

Most vulnerable were financial institutions in little podunk towns with only a sheriff or two to protect them. Texas is big and sprawling and full of such towns, which made easy pickings for bank robbers.

Unfortunately, the TBA's $5000 reward inspired some unscrupulous people to trick others into robbing banks for them. There were many variations on this scheme, but they all ended with the perpetrators being killed by their "friends" who would then collect the reward. There are even accounts of corrupt cops taking part in such shenanigans.

In response, the TBA said that even if a person had been duped into robbing a bank, they were still a bank robber and deserved their fate. They did, however, amend the wording for the Dead Bank Robber Reward Program ever so slightly, by adding that from that point on the bounty only applied towards, "legally killed robbers."

The Santa Claus Robber of Cisco

Now, let's get back to our tale of a Santa Claus gone bad. Shortly after being paroled for bank robbery in the town of Valera, Texas, Marshall Ratliff decided to strike again. This time, his target would be the First National Bank in Cisco, Texas.

Ratliff had lived in Cisco prior to going to jail and the local sheriff G.E. "Bit" Bedford had helped put him away for his earlier crime. Not wanting to be recognized by Bedford or any other local citizens, Ratliff donned a Santa outfit before heading to town in a stolen car along with his three accomplices.

Shortly after noon on December 23, 1927 a deviant "Santa," sauntered down Main Street in Cisco, Texas while his companions parked the getaway car in an alley. By the time Ratliff stepped into the First National Bank, he had several children in tow.

"Hello, Santa!" a bank teller called out upon seeing him. Ratliff did not reply, so the teller repeated his greeting.

Moments later, Santa's little helpers burst through the door, but instead of spreading Christmas cheer, the trio brandished guns. As one told the cashier to put his hands up, the other two forced bank workers to open the safe. Meanwhile, Santa/Ratliff began stuffing a large sack with money.

Yes, Frances, there is a Santa Claus

In the midst of all this, a 6-year-old girl named Frances who had seen Santa earlier convinced her mom, Mrs. B.P. Blassengame, to take her into the bank to meet Santa.

Mrs. Blassengame quickly realized what was really going on, and even though Santa threatened to shoot if she did not stay put, she bravely grabbed little Frances, charged through the middle of the bank and straight out the back door.

Along the way, she warned employees in the bank's back offices of the robbery in progress. Mrs. Blassengame quickly shuffled Frances off to safety then ran down the alley to the police department, yelling the whole way in order to warn others of the robbery.

Shootout Sparks Surge in Gun Sales

As soon as the police arrived on the scene, bullets began to fly. It's unclear exactly how the shootout began, but it was intense. Remember that Dead Robber Reward Program?

Once word spread that a bank robbery was in progress, what began as a shootout between the four robbers and a trio of local law enforcement agents quickly ballooned into a huge gun battle involving many of Cisco's citizens, some of whom were already armed with pistols or rifles. Those who weren't, including a couple postal workers, ran to the local hardware store to buy guns and ammo so they could join in!

It must have been like a scene out of a Quentin Tarantino movie. Over 200 bullet holes were counted in the bank. Who knows how many shots were fired in the subsequent chase and shootouts along the way?

Robbers Foiled by their own Stupidity

As bullets flew, the robbers forced the customers out of the bank, keeping two little girls aged 10 and 12 as hostages as they fled in their getaway car. Sadly, both the police chief and his deputy later died from wounds received in this barrage. Six other citizens were injured. Shortly after the getaway car sped off, the robbers realized that they had forgotten an important detail – to fill the gas tank!

In addition, one of their tires was flattened by a shot from the pursuing mob. At the edge of town, they carjacked a passing Oldsmobile driven by a fourteen-year-old named Woodrow Wilson Harris.

Only after grabbing the loot, the hostages, and then scrambling into their newly-commandeered getaway vehicle – while under fire from the approaching mob – did the bandits realize that Woodrow Wilson Harris had cleverly taken the ignition keys with him as he ran off!

By this time, one of the four robbers, who had taken a bullet early on, lapsed into unconsciousness. The remaining robbers left him behind as they piled back into their original getaway car.

As they once again sped off, the group came to a startling realization: not only had they left their wounded companion behind, but the entire $12,400 they had stolen from the bank, as well.

In desperation, the fugitives drove off the dirt road until the cactus, scrub oak, and mesquite became too thick for them to continue. Exasperated, the three remaining criminals decided to leave the car and their hostages behind and stumble on by foot.

As word of the crime spread, a huge manhunt ensued, with citizen volunteers and law enforcement joining in. When the trio of robbers was finally apprehended, Ratliff's Santa suit had no less than six bullet holes in it, and they were all quite wounded and weak.

Santa Claus Robber Brought to Trial

All three eventually stood trial. Of Santa's remaining helpers, one was quickly executed in the electric chair, and the other sentenced to 99 years in prison. After the latter was paroled in the 1940's, he changed his name, and presumably became a law abiding citizen. (Hey, we can hope!)

As for Marshall Ratliff, a.k.a. the Santa Claus robber, he was convicted of armed robbery on January 27, 1928, and sentenced to 99 years in prison. In March, however, he was additionally sentenced to execution for his role in the deaths of the police chief and his deputy.

Santa Feigns Insanity

Ratliff responded by unsuccessfully feigning insanity. As hard as he tried, folks found it just a little too convenient that all of his symptoms appeared the moment he learned of his death sentence. While awaiting execution in Eastland, however, Ratliff's health declined and he became paralyzed. This health condition meant that his jailers had to feed, bathe and help Ratliff use the toilet. It was all a ruse, however.

One evening, as two jailers were taking care of him, Ratliff suddenly grabbed a gun from a nearby desk and shot one of them to death. A fist fight ensued between Ratliff and the remaining jailer.

The gunshot caught the attention of passersby. They rushed to the scene but were unable to get into the locked cell to help. All they could do was watch as the pair engaged in a lengthy knockdown, drag out fight. Eventually, the jailer managed to knock Ratliff unconscious and shove him back into his cell.

Bad Santa Lynched in Eastland

Even though the jailer told the onlookers to go home, the townspeople were infuriated. By morning, a crowd of 2000 plus people gathered in front of the jail. The jailer was overwhelmed by a rush of angry vigilantes who stormed the jail and dragged Ratliff out.

Shortly after, the Santa Claus Robber was strung up between two telephone poles and hung by the neck until dead. Ironically, the site of his lynching was behind the Majestic Theater where a play called, "The Noose," was currently running.

While no one was ever charged for Ratliff's lynching (big surprise, eh?) the Dead Bank Robber Reward Program was eventually phased out - but not until 1964.

Eastland Law Enforcement Museum

The jailhouse where all this craziness went down is now a museum dedicated to Eastland County's law enforcement history, of which there is plenty. Here you can see where Marshall Ratliff carved his name on the wall of his cell, and the actual rope that was used to lynch him, among other exhibits.

Plan your trip to the Eastland Law Enforcement Museum
Website: eastlandfoundation.com/lawEnforcement.html
Address: 210 W. White St., Eastland, TX 76488

Mural Made from Postage Stamps

Marene Johnson Johnson, who was Eastland's Postmistress from 1957 - 1968, spent her free time creating a mural made entirely from postage stamps, 11,217 of them to be exact. This unique work of art measures 6 by 10 feet and uses stamps to depict Benjamin Franklin, Martha Washington, Abe Lincoln, the United Nations Emblem, and more.

The project took Johnson 7 years to complete at a cost of $15,000 worth of stamps, and she donated it to the post office when she was finished. In 1988, the stamps in the mural were estimated to be worth 5 million dollars. Today you can view this one-of-a-kind piece of art for free simply by swinging by the Eastland Texas Post Office.

Plan your trip to Eastland's Postage Stamp Mural
Address: Eastland Post Office, 411 W. Main Street, Eastland, TX 76488

EULESS

Garden of Angels Murder Memorial

At their trial, Carolyn Barker was horrified to hear two men not only confess to killing her granddaughter, but remark that they hoped to get famous for the deed. That's when she decided something is wrong with society's glorification of murderers, and that it is their victims who should be celebrated and remembered.

Barker placed a small white cross in memory of Amy Robinson, her 19-year-old granddaughter, in the area where her body was discovered by police. Soon, other crosses appeared. As of 2013, 102 white crosses stand in memory of Texas murder victims.

As someone who enjoys perusing historic cemeteries, of which Texas has many, I must say that The Garden of Angels murder memorial feels very different. I found it sobering and emotional. It was jarring to realize that while I know the names of many famous murderers, from Jack the

Ripper to John Wayne Gacey, I know very little about their victims.

Annual Charity Events

Since The Garden of Angels is a non-profit memorial park for murder victims, they occasionally host charity events such as toy drives at Christmas, memorial services, and even up-beat get togethers with live music and snacks.

While I wouldn't call a trip to The Garden of Angels entertaining, it is a beautiful setting, and I could see and feel how it can provides solace for those who have lost loved ones through violence. I found it serene and meditative, and walked away feeling very fortunate.

Plan your trip to the Garden of Angels Murder Memorial
Website: ourgardenofangels.org
Address: 11271 Mossier Valley Road, Euless, Texas 76040

FORT WORTH

Overview of Fort Worth

Fort Worth is often referred to as "Where the West begins" and not simply because it sits a good 35 miles west of Dallas. Unlike the Big D, Fort Worth unabashedly embraces its cowboy roots, carrying its "wild west" atmosphere straight into the 21st century. Nowhere is this influence more apparent than in the part of town known as the Stockyards.

I found a lot of offbeat and overlooked things in Fort Worth: a tree with buried treasure beneath it, a beer can house, the only Michelangelo painting in the western hemisphere, a wax version of The Last Supper, and much more. But before we get to that, let's talk about the city of Fort Worth's official longhorn herd.

History of the Fort Worth Stockyards

Shortly after the Civil War, Fort Worth became a popular pit stop for cowboys driving their cattle up through Texas. These "drovers," as the men were called, often stopped in Fort Worth for supplies. The city became so popular with cattlemen that they christened it "Cowtown," an affectionate nickname that endures to this day.

Up until the mid-1950's, the Fort Worth Stockyards was a major hub for the livestock industry, a place where cattle, pigs, and sheep were bought, sold and slaughtered. For many years, it was the biggest livestock market south of Kansas City.

The Fort Worth Stockyards Daily Cattle Drives

The livestock market may be gone, but the cattle drive lives on. Twice each day, Fort Worth's city herd of 15 longhorns saunters down East Exchange Avenue, right in front of the Livestock Exchange Building.

There are lots of places to watch the daily cattle drives. You can simply stand on the sidewalk, or the lawn in front of the Livestock Exchange Building. If you want to take pictures, find a section of sidewalk where there isn't a big car or SUV in front of you because people are not allowed in the street. I stepped into the street with my camera and was quickly herded back onto the sidewalk with the rest of my species.

If your heart isn't set on snapping photos, then sitting at any restaurant with outdoor seating along East Exchange

Avenue is also a fun way to enjoy this twice daily event. Some words of advice: Be on time! Longhorn cattle are not slow pokes. These steer were bred for walking all day long, so a short jaunt down the street only takes them a few minutes.

You can visit these longhorns in their corral behind the Livestock Exchange Building before and after the daily cattle drives. While there, keep an eye out for drovers, dressed in 19th century garb, who are happy to pose for pictures with you and answer questions about life in the old west.

Plan your trip to the Fort Worth Stockyards
Website: www.fortworthstockyards.org
Address: East Exchange Avenue, Fort Worth, TX 76164.

The Eternal Light of Fort Worth

Fort Worth, Texas is home to the second longest lasting light bulb in the world. Nicknamed the "Eternal Light," this legendary light bulb has been burning since September 21, 1908.

Now on view at the Fort Worth Stockyards Museum, where it is protected from the harsh Texas elements and kept on a protected electrical circuit, this little 4-watt wonder started out on the back porch of the Byers Opera House, which later became the Palace Theater. The name of the joint really didn't matter to the bulb, of course, it simply kept burning… and burning… and burning!

Second Longest Lasting Light Bulb in the World

As early as 1928, people began to marvel over the longevity of this particular light bulb. For a bulb to burn for two decades seemed pretty amazing. Little did they know it would keep on going for over a century.

In 1970, *The Guinness Book of World Records* listed the Fort Worth light as the longest burning bulb in the world. It was bumped to second place, however, in 1973 by The Centennial Light, which burns in a Livermore, California fire station, and boasts its own webcam. Even in second place, I think the Eternal Light of Fort Worth, Texas is mighty impressive.

Plan Your Trip to the Stockyards Museum
Website: stockyardsmuseum.org
Address: 131 E Exchange Ave #113, Fort Worth, TX 76164

Fort Worth Water Gardens

The Fort Worth Water Gardens are a modern take on ancient city fountains, with Mother Nature as the theme instead of cherubs and Roman gods. Built in 1974 by prestigious architects, Philip Johnson and John Burgee, this park covers 4.3 acres smack in the middle of downtown Fort Worth. Even though flanked by skyscrapers and Interstate 30, it successfully creates a contemplative oasis in the middle of a busy urban environment. Best of all, this peaceful space is free to the public and open every single day.

The park is divided into four unique spaces:

The Active Pool

The Fort Worth Water Gardens "Active Pool" is a spiral labyrinth of stepping stones leading down to a small pool in the center. Water rushes down from a height of nearly four stories on all sides, creating roaring white noise and mist. On a hot Texas day (of which we have many), that mist is quite refreshing.

The cascading water of the Active Pool creates a confusing sensation of movement as you hop down the steps. There are no handrails - so tread carefully. Sure, in the 1975 movie "Logan's Run," the main character is seen racing through this area, but I suggest watching your step. If you have kids, or any problems with your balance, caution is key. In fact, even if you have no physical issues at all, be careful here.

The Aerating Pool

The Aerating Pool features an evenly spaced array of sprinklers. This can be a beautiful, rainbow-filled sight when the lighting is right. It can also be frustrating on a hot day because wading is not allowed and all those sprinklers are just begging for someone to go galloping through them in a bathing suit. Oh well. Sometimes, we must suffer to enjoy art.

The Quiet Pool

The Fort Worth Water Gardens' "Quiet Pool," is exactly that, quiet, languid and serene. It's the type of place that makes you start whispering even though it's not required. Something about the smooth surface of this large rectangular pool takes the rowdiness right out of you. This meditative pool is a good spot to sit and sketch, read a book, or maybe even steal a kiss from your sweetheart.

This large rectangular pool is rimmed by cypress trees, which create beautiful shadows on the water-streaked walls of the perimeter. The knobby "cypress knees" crowding around the base of each tree remind me of vigilant little prairie dogs.

The Mountain

This is the only section of the Fort Worth Water Gardens which does not feature water. The narrow ledges, created well before today's rock-climbing walls, are meant to simulate the feeling of climbing a mountain. I must admit that, since I have only visited the park on hot days, I rarely spend much time here. In cooler weather, I will give it a climb.

Movies Filmed at the Fort Worth Water Gardens

As I mentioned earlier, the Active Pool is featured in a chase scene in the 1975 sci-fi flick "Logan's Run." It also appears in the ending of the 1979 TV version of another sci-fi movie, "The Lathe of Heaven." I can see why directors choose this space for scenes. There is something about the Fort Worth Water Gardens that can make your imagination run wild, even if you're not a sci-fi buff.

Plan your trip to the Fort Worth Water Gardens
Address: 1502 Commerce St, Fort Worth, TX 76102

Only Michelangelo Painting in the Western Hemisphere

When I first moved to Texas, I figured local museums would mainly feature paintings with cowboys, Indians and longhorns, so I was pleasantly surprised to discover that

North Texas museums have well-rounded collections featuring a wide variety of art – from ancient times up through the present. Fort Worth, in fact, is home to the only Michelangelo painting in the western hemisphere.

The painting, filled with fascinating-yet-creepy creatures, was painted by Michelangelo Buonarotti around 1487 or 1488, when was only 12 or 13 years old. It's called "The Torment of Saint Anthony" and was inspired by an engraving by Martin Schongauer. Michelangelo did more than just copy Schongauer's engraving. He added interesting anatomical details, such as fish scales, to the myriad demonic creatures seen pestering the saint. Michelangelo, of course, is more famous for his sculptures (such as the Pieta and David) than his paintings. He is only known to have created four paintings in his lifetime.

"The Torment of Saint Anthony" now hangs in the Kimbell Art Museum of Fort Worth, Texas. It's in the viewing area that is free to the public.

Plan your trip to the Kimbell Art Museum
Website: kimbellart.org
Address: 3333 Camp Bowie Blvd, Fort Worth, TX 76107

Lee Harvey Oswald's Grave

Since no cemetery in Dallas would take him, the body of President John F. Kennedy's assassin wound up in Shannon Rose Hill Cemetery of Fort Worth. It is even claimed that so few people attended Lee Harvey Oswald's funeral that journalists covering the story were enlisted as pall bearers.

Oswald's grave is marked by a small rectangular slab that is flush to the ground. It bears no dates or other information, not even the man's full name. The stone simply reads, "Oswald."

Finding Oswald's grave can be somewhat tricky, especially since cemetery officials no longer give directions to any of their internments. If you decide to go, be aware that the graveyard is divided into sections marked by stenciled labels on the curb. As you head to the west, keep an eye out for the section labeled "Sunset 18." Look nearby for a mausoleum marked Shannon. As you stand in front of it, you will need to walk around it on the left side. Oswald's marker is about 20 feet behind this mausoleum. It's to the right of a tree, and the grass in front of it has been worn bare.

The Mystery of Nick Beef

In 1997, a new grave marker mysteriously appeared next to Lee Harvey Oswald's. Not only is it the same size and shape as Oswald's, but like his, this marker is not inscribed with any dates or information beyond a name, "Nick Beef."

Up until then, the tangled web of conspiracy theories surrounding the Kennedy assassination bore no mention of a man by this name. When people looked into the matter, they were unable to learn much about the mysterious Mr. Beef's life, death, or any possible connections to Lee Harvey Oswald. The story I ran across most frequently claims that two local reporters (or historians, depending on the version) placed the Nick Beef marker beside Oswald's so that visitors could find it more easily.

Even if this were true, it still begs the question: Who is Nick Beef? In 2013 the *New York Times* got to the bottom of things by interviewing the mysterious Nick Beef who, it turns out, is alive and well.

Nick Beef is the alter ego of a man named Patric Abedin, who describes himself as a writer and "nonperforming performance artist." Mr. Abedin grew up in Texas. He was in elementary school when Kennedy was shot, and has vivid memories of seeing the president and First

Lady when they arrived at the airport in 1963. As a child, he and his mother often dropped by Oswald's grave.

In 1975, Abedin heard that the plot beside Oswald's was unclaimed, so he dropped by the cemetery and purchased it for himself. He then moved to New York, got married, had kids, found work as a humor writer, and made a life for himself there.

When Mr. Abedin's mother passed away in late 1996, he returned to Texas for the memorial. That's when, on a whim, he purchased the grave marker. Not wanting to expose his kids to any inquiries, he had the little stone inscribed with his pen name, "Nick Beef," instead of his given name. When the interviewer asked why he had purchased the plot, and later the marker, Abedin was rather cryptic. In both cases, it was an impulse buy, one with motives that are not only difficult for him to verbalize, but seem to be a mystery even to himself. To add to the oddness, Mr. Abedin has no plans to ever be buried there. When his time comes, he wants to be cremated.

Plan your trip to Shannon Rose Hill Cemetery
Address: 7301 East Lancaster, Fort Worth, TX 76112

Rooftop Jackalope Sculpture

Jackalopes are mythical rabbit/antelope hybrids that frequently appear in folk tales from the southwestern United States. In the 1980's, Fort Worth artist Nancy Lamb was commissioned to create an 8-foot tall jackalope sculpture for a garden and pottery shop. Although the Jackalope Store has since gone under, its unique mascot remains on the roof of what is now a car dealership.

Plan your trip to the Rooftop Jackalope
Address: 5925 Camp Bowie Blvd., Fort Worth, TX

Life Sized Last Supper Replica Made from Wax

In 1955, an oil tycoon named Bill Fleming commissioned a version of Leonardo Da Vinci's masterpiece, The Last Supper. However, instead of a painting, Fleming paid for a life-sized sculpture made from wax. The Fort Worth man had seen a "wax supper" in California and wanted to give his hometown something similar.

To complete this project, Fleming hired the mother-daughter team of Katherine and Katherine Marie Stubergh, a duo well-known for their wax sculptures. The younger Stubergh originally planned to be a dancer. Even so, as a teenager, she produced a wax sculpture of Mae West. West was so impressed with the result that she allegedly told the girl, "Kid, anybody can make a piece of mud look like me shouldn't be no dancer." From that point on, the younger Stubergh ditched her dancing dreams to pursue art full force.

Fort Worth's wax supper took the Stuberghs 18 months to create. It was finished in 1956 and displayed in various locations, from churches to a shopping mall, over the next 40 years. In 1997, it was placed in storage, and for a while, all seemed lost. In 2009, however, the wax display was restored. As of this writing, the Stubergh's wax supper is on display at the Christian Arts Museum in Fort Worth, Texas.

Plan your trip to the Christian Arts Museum
Address: 3221 Hamilton Ave., Fort Worth, TX

Annual Oscar® Watching Party at The Modern

Every year, DFW.com, The Modern, and the Lone Star Film Society host an Oscar Watching Party at the Modern Art Museum of Fort Worth, Texas. This free event is much better than sitting at home watching the gala event on TV. Why should west coast VIP's have all the fun?

For one thing, the people-watching is top notch. Not only will you see snappy tuxedos and glittering gowns galore, but many people dress as their favorite movie characters, past and present.

Papparazzi and journalists greet you at the entrance, interview everyone, and snap red carpet photos of every single 'celebrity' who walks through the door - including you. They will also ask questions such as who you think will win Best Actor, and what designer you are wearing. (As to the latter query, I'm nearly always attired by Thrift Town.)

The first year I attended, I worried the event might attract an insular crowd, some impenetrable clique of film snobs, but that was not the case. This is Cowtown, after all, not the real Hollywood. People were friendly, and we had lively conversations all evening. An open bar, snacks, and a slew of generous prizes, rounded out the offerings.

The bottom line is that this annual Oscar watching party is just that – a party! Sure, you can sit in the auditorium and not miss a thing, but if you find your attention wandering, you can walk out into the other section to mix and mingle. They even give away prizes during commercials.

Plan your trip to the Oscar® Watching Party
Website: themodern.org
Address: Modern Art Museum of Fort Worth, 3200 Darnell Street, Fort Worth, Texas 76107

Fort Worth Beer Can House

It's always beer-thirty over at 2901 Whitmore Street in Fort Worth, Texas. That's where Louis Torres began stringing up empty cans of beer in his trees. Some of these glittery garlands have been slit and squashed just enough to make them resemble Christmas ornaments, while others remain intact. Mr. Torres only uses Miller Lite and Milwaukee's Best Light, so there's a cohesive color scheme to his creation.

From a distance the Fort Worth Beer Can House reminded me of an orchard overtaken by webworm, but as you get closer, it's a pretty sight. A slight breeze on the day I drove by added to the dreamy ambience as hundreds of shiny cans swayed gently.

Beer Donations Welcome

Mr. Torres started his beer can house a few years ago, and it not only keeps him busy, but he often comes home to cases of beer on his front porch from anonymous donors. Other times, fellow beer drinkers will come by when he's home and share a few brewskis with him as part of their contribution to the project. One anonymous patron sent him a neon beer sign.

It's interesting to note that Mr. Torres does not consider his house a work of art. For him, it's simply a fun pastime.

Gold Buried Beneath a Fort Worth Tree

Seceding from the United States was not an easy decision for the State of Texas, and many Texans, including Charles Turner (1822-1873) a farmer, merchant, and Texas Ranger, were against it. Even so, once the state voted to withdraw from the Union, Mr. Turner reluctantly went along with it – up to a point.

While Charles Turner showed his support of secession by funding a company of volunteer soldiers with his own money, he balked at the idea of exchanging his hard-earned fortune for Confederate notes, which is why he ended up burying an alleged $10,000 in gold beneath an oak tree on his farm.

A Wise Investment

Money may not grow on trees, but it doesn't depreciate when buried beneath one. After the Civil War, when Confederate notes were worthless, Charles Turner returned to his farm and dug up his buried treasure. He then used it to help Fort Worth, a young city struggling to build its infrastructure and pay back northern creditors.

Though now considered one of the founders of Fort Worth, Charles Turner has long since "bought the farm" as we humans tend to do. The oak tree that kept watch over his buried treasure lives on. The area that was once Mr. Turner's farm is now a well-kept and rather upscale cemetery called Greenwood Memorial Park.

Living History: A Bicentennial Tree

There are two plaques at the base of this majestic Texas Live Oak, a.k.a. *Quercus fusiformis* if you want to get technical. One plaque describes the history of this famous tree which is now known as the Turner Oak. The other, placed by the Daughters of the Revolution, explains that since this beautiful oak was alive when the United States Constitution was signed, it has also earned the title of Bicentennial Tree.

How to Find the Turner Oak

If you would like to visit the Turner Oak, and I highly recommend that you do, head over to Greenwood Memorial Park in Fort Worth. This famous tree is located in a traffic circle shortly after the main entrance. It is situated directly behind the first Greenwood Memorial Park sign you see as you drive into the graveyard.

Plan your trip to the Turner Oak
Address: Greenwood Memorial Park, 3100 White Settlement Rd, Fort Worth, TX 76107

GLEN ROSE

Glen Rose Overview

For a city with a mere 2,500 inhabitants, there is a surprising amount of fun things to see and do in Glen Rose. Like so many north Texas towns it features a historic square ringed by mom and pop stores. Keep in mind that if you visit on a Sunday, most will be closed.

Petrified Wood Buildings in Texas

In the late 1920's, several Texas cities, including Austin, Huntville, and Stephenville, used petrified wood as a decorative building material. Sadly, only a handful of these unique structures remain. In its hey-day, the local chamber of commerce nicknamed Glen Rose "Petrified City" because it had at least 65 buildings constructed from petrified wood. Of these, about 40 remain, which is considerably more than anywhere else.

Glen Rose Historic Town Square

Compared to other Texas cities with historic courthouse squares, the one in Glen Rose is quite petite. That said, bigger is not always better, even in Texas.

The Glen Rose town square includes unique details that set it apart from others I have seen. At the center is Somervell Courthouse, a beautiful building in the Romanesque Revival style, which dates from 1894. There is a little park in front of it which features a gazebo and a star-shaped water fountain, both of which are made from locally found petrified wood, crystals, and fossilized mud with dinosaur footprints.

Look to your left as you face Somervell Courthouse, and you find a bronze sculpture which depicts a woman on horseback reaching out towards a cowboy. The plaque beside it describes a fascinating true story, a romantic tale in which a young Hispanic woman captured by Native Americans is rescued, then falls in love with a cowboy. After riding off into the sunset, the pair (Charles and Juana Barnard) founded the town of Glen Rose and had fourteen children together.

Shopping in Downtown Glen Rose

Somervell Courthouse is surrounded by cute little shops. Glance down the street and you'll notice that the hardware store is a hangout for local guys, especially the silver-haired set. A little farther down the street you will find a marvelous cafe.

Plan your trip to Historic Downtown Glen Rose
Address: Somervell Courthouse, 101 NE Barnard St, Glen Rose, Texas 76043

Storiebook Café

I was delighted to discover that the only bookstore in town is also home to a charming café. I fell in love with the Storiebook Café the moment I stepped inside, thanks to the creative décor, the bookshelves with sliding ladders, and – more than anything else – the friendly vibe. Luckily, the food did not disappoint. It was too hot for coffee, but the Greek salad and iced tea I had were light and refreshing.

Plan your trip to Storiebook Café
Website: storiebookcafe.com
Address: 502 NE Barnard Street, Glen Rose, Texas 76043

Barnard Street Bakery

My other big foodie thrill in Glen Rose was stumbling upon an excellent bakery in – of all places – a gas station. We stopped on our way into town and as I poked around looking for iced tea, I noticed some beautiful pastries for sale. By "beautiful" I mean it was obvious that they were baked from scratch. (Full disclosure: I owned a bakery/coffeehouse for a few years, so I have an eye for these things.) We bought a brownie and it was fantastic. As a result, not only did we stop in for fresh pastries the next morning, but we left town with a bag full for the road.

Plan your trip to Barnard Street Bakery
Website: tigercorner.net
Address: Tiger Corner – Exxon, 1110 NE Big Bend Trail, Glen Rose, TX 76043

Big Rocks Park

As the name suggests, there are a lot of big rocks to be found at Big Rocks Park. It's still an understatement, somehow, because there is more to these huge stones than just their size. I think it's fascinating how the river has sculpted them into smooth, sinuous shapes, rather like petrified clouds.

The boulders are fun to climb on, and when the river is up, people also swim and raft here. I visited during a drought, however, so the riverbed was nearly dry. Even so, it's a fun place to let your kids run off some steam after being cooped up in the car for a while and makes a good backdrop for family photos. Plus, it's free.

Plan your trip to Big Rocks Park
Address: 1014 SW Barnard Street, Glen Rose, Texas 76043

Oakdale Park 1930's motor court

The City of Glen Rose recently purchased Oakdale Park, a humble remnant of 1930's vacation history. Back in the 20's and 30's, Americans started traveling for pleasure. Enterprising folks saw a need for shelter along major roadways, and soon, little cabins cropped up along the way to provide this. Each of Oakdale Park's little cabins are available for rental. In addition, the pool here is quite large, even by today's standards, and for a small fee you can take a dip even if you are not staying in a cabin.

Plan your trip to Oakdale Park
Website: oakdalepark.com
Address: 1019 NE Barnard St, Glen Rose, TX 76043

Fossil Rim Wildlife Center

For those who want to see exotic animals up close, Fossil Rim Wildlife Center is a safari park with over 1,000 African and Asian animals. Visitors can choose to drive through on their own or take guided tours. In hot weather, get to the park early since many animals retreat to the shade during mid-day. The animals are accustomed to people and will approach your vehicle hoping for snacks. There is a café halfway through, however, it's a good idea to also bring your own snacks and water so you won't be rushed.

Plan your trip to Fossil Rim Wildlife Center
Website: fossilrim.org
Address: 2299 County Road 2008, Glen Rose, TX 76043

Dinosaur Valley State Park

This being Texas, our state dinosaur isn't just big, it is arguably the largest creature to have ever to walked the earth. Another great thing about our dino is that you don't have to visit a museum to see evidence of its existence. Much like the famous movie star handprints in front of Grauman's Chinese in Los Angeles, *Pauluxysaurus Jonesi* left footprints all over Glen Rose and its surroundings.

A trip to Glen Rose isn't complete without paying homage to this big critter. A great place to do so is at Dinosaur Valley State Park, where the Pauluxy River's clay-like mud perfectly preserves several of the huge creature's footprints. When the river is low, these ancient footprints are easy to see. If the river is up, you may have to get your feet wet, but it's definitely worth it

Plan your trip to Dinosaur Valley State Park
Official website: tpwd.state.tx.us/state-parks/dinosaur-valley
Address: 1629 Park Road 59, Glen Rose, Texas 76043

Dinosaur World

Parents, be warned! On your way to Dinosaur Valley State Park, you will pass extremely tempting child bait in the form of a place called Dinosaur World. This 22-acre park features over 100 life-sized dinosaur models, as well as a museum, a playground, and even a place where kids can dig for fossils. If your pockets are deep, or you have a kid with dinosaur-fever, it is worth visiting. If you are on a tight budget, rest assured that there are two large dinosaur statues within the state park that will definitely delight the little ones.

Plan your trip to Dinosaur World
Website: dinosaurworld.com
Address: 1058 Park Road 59 Glen Rose, TX 76043

Best Western Dinosaur Valley Inn

My husband and I stayed at the Best Western Dinosaur Valley Inn and Suites on this particular trip, and it exceeded all expectations. Not only were the accommodations clean and comfortable, but the free breakfast, while simple, included plenty of options. The outdoor pools are refreshing and include a shaded swimming area, which is important here in Texas. The dinosaur-themed decor works well, with the koi pond adding a touch of elegance. The staff was helpful and, unlike so many places offering free wireless Internet, the Wi-Fi at this hotel worked great.

Plan your trip to Best Western Dinosaur Valley Inn
Website: dinosaurvalleyinn.com
Address: 1311 NE Big Bend Trail, Glen Rose, TX 76043

GRANBURY

Overview of Granbury

Granbury is a small but lively town which hosts one festival after another throughout the year, including a kite festival, a Texas Independence Day Celebration, a Wine Walk, and a Warriors for Christ biker rally in the fall, among several others. It's also home to some quirky history and conspiracy theories, so let's get those out of the way first:

Granbury Folklore, History and Conspiracy Theories

What do John Wilkes Booth, Billy the Kid, and Jesse James have in common? All three outlaws have links to Granbury, Texas where they are rumored to have faked their own deaths.

In a story so strange that it's been covered by the likes of the TV shows "20/20" and "Unsolved Mysteries," some folks seriously believe that Abraham Lincoln's assassin was not killed after his crime, but fled to Texas, where he lived a long life.

According to the story, Booth took the name "John St. Helen" and quietly tended bar in Granbury for many years until becoming ill. He was so sick that in what he considered a deathbed confession, Booth/St. Helen admitted to killing President Lincoln. Much to his surprise he got better, but with his cover blown he had no choice but to split town. According to this story, Booth settled in Enid, Oklahoma where he committed suicide in 1903. Instead of receiving a burial, his body was mummified and paraded around the country as part of a carnival sideshow. These days, a mural depicting him tending bar inside the Nutt House (a bakery on Granbury's town square) is a reminder of this strange tale.

Another odd claim is that Jesse James was not actually killed in St. Joseph, Missouri in 1882 as we have all been led to believe. No, the real Jesse James died of natural causes at the ripe old age of 103 after spending the remainder of his life in Granbury, Texas. There is even a grave in the local cemetery which reads, "CSA - Jesse Woodson James. Sept. 5, 1847-Aug.15, 1951. Supposedly killed in 1882." So who is in the grave labeled "Jesse James" back in Kearney, Missouri? According to this tale, a man named Charles Bigelow took a hit so that Mr. James could have a fresh start.

While it seems that a DNA test could get to the bottom of this tale faster than you can say "Maury Povich," the situation remains unclear. Even though a DNA test from 2000 shows that the fellow in Granbury is not Jesse James, some locals claim that the wrong body was exhumed for the exam. As recently as 2013, a request to perform DNA tests on the body in Kearny, Missouri was declined.

As for Billy the Kid, the Granbury connection is more tenuous, but it's still enough to make you scratch your head. The official story is that Billy the Kid was shot and killed in Fort Sumner, New Mexico in 1881. Once again, however, many claim that the sheriff mistakenly shot a different man, but claimed it was Billy the Kid, to make himself look good.

The legend continues with Kid traveling to Granbury in 1949 to attend Jesse James 102nd birthday party. A year later, when this Billy the Kid died of a heart attack, the gravestone for him in New Mexico went missing. It stayed missing until 1976 when it turned up in, you guessed it, the city of Granbury, Texas.

Rebecca Crockett's Grave at Acton State Historic Site

History buffs will want to swing by Acton Cemetery on their way to or from Granbury, since it's only 10 minutes from town. Acton is a beautiful and well-maintained historic graveyard with some of the largest pecan trees I have ever seen.

In addition to several Civil War era headstones, you can't help but notice the 28-foot marble statue at Rebecca Crockett's gravesite. From 1949 until 2007 this was considered the smallest state park in Texas, but in 2008 it was designated a state historic site.

Rebecca Crockett is the second wife of the legendary folk hero, Davy Crockett, who died at the Alamo. After his death, she moved to north Texas with her children hoping to stake claim to land she had inherited through his government service.

Although Rebecca Crockett died in 1860, it wasn't until 1911 that the marble monument was erected in her honor. It's a pretty statue, depicting a pioneer woman wearing a bonnet and shading her eyes as she gazes to the west.

Recently, an annual Rebecca Crockett memorial service, complete with fiddle players and attendants wearing period clothing, has been organized for Texas Independence Day in March. Keep an eye on the Acton State Historic Site website for details of upcoming events.

Plan your trip to Acton Cemetery
Website: visitactontx.com
Address: Acton Cemetery, FM 167, Acton, TX 76049

Granbury's Historic Town Square

Granbury's stately native limestone courthouse is a fine example of French Empire Style architecture and dates back to 1891. The courthouse is flanked by dozens of mom and pop stores, restaurants, and cafes. During festivals, this area turns into an outdoor fair with bandstands and booths selling arts and crafts.

Plan your trip to Granbury's Historic Town Square
Address: 100 E Pearl St, Granbury, TX 76048

Family Theatre and Drive-In

If you plan to spend an evening there, check out the Granbury Theatre Company for family-friendly plays and musicals. For for a taste of 20th century history, try the Brazos Drive-In. This family-run operation has been in the same location for the past 50+ years and is open year-round.

Plan your trip to the Granbury Theatre
Website: granburytheatrecompany.org
Address: 133 East Pearl Street, Granbury, TX 76048

Plan your trip to the Brazos Drive-in
Website: thebrazos.com
Address: Brazos Drive-in, 1800 W. Pearl Street, Granbury, TX 76048

Windmill Farm

As you leave Granbury, set your GPS for the Windmill Farm. Even if you do not choose to spend the night at this bed and breakfast, it is free of charge to take photos as you drive through their charming collection of over 40 decorative windmills.

Plan your trip to the Windmill Farm
Website: thewindmillfarm.com
Address: Windmill Farm & Bed & Breakfast, 6625 Colony Road, Tolar, TX 76476

GRAND SALINE

Salt Palace in Grand Saline

While the French equivalent of "window shopping" translates as "window licking," this is something that literally occurs every day at the Salt Palace in Grand Saline, Texas. This odd building, which houses a visitor center and museum for the town and the nearby Morton Salt Company mine, is built entirely out of salt crystal bricks held together by a salt/mortar mixture. This strange combination proves tempting to many visitors who satisfy their curiosity by taking a tiny lick of its walls.

The building now standing is the third incarnation of this salty enterprise. The first "Salt Palace" (shack, would be a more accurate moniker) was a mock-up of The Alamo created for the 1936 Texas Centennial Celebration. Texas weather being what it is, the building eventually eroded. Another Salt Palace was built in 1975 by local citizens who also created the first annual Salt Festival which continues to be held every year on the second weekend of June.

Heavy rain took its toll on Salt Palace number two, so in 1993 a third version was erected. This time, an aluminum overhang was added to protect it from the elements. While it's an impressive site, the name, "Salt Palace" is a bit grandiose for the little one-story building that bears the name.

Salt Palace Museum

Grand Saline has had a salt factory since 1839 and during the Civil War the factory supplied the Confederacy with 500 pounds of salt per day. Around 1920, Morton Salt stepped in and the little girl with the yellow umbrella took over. Miners harvest salt from 750 feet below ground in the remnants of an ancient sea that covered east Texas 250 million years ago. Grand Saline's mines contain a large and high-quality salt deposit. It's been estimated to contain enough salt to supply the entire world for the next 20,000 years.

Tours of the nearby Morton Salt mines are no longer available due to safety regulations enacted in the 1960's, but the Salt Palace houses a museum which offers a movie showing mining production, mining artifacts and other historic memorabilia.

Famous Aviator from Grand Saline

Some of the museum's exhibits are devoted to Wiley Post, the famed aviator who grew up on a farm in Grand Saline. Despite losing an eye in an oil field accident, Post went on to set two world records for flights around the world as well as being the first pilot to enter the stratosphere. Unfortunately, Post and legendary comedienne, Will Rogers, died together in a plane crash in Alaska in 1935.

Grand Saline Salt Fest

Each June, the town of Grand Saline hosts its annual Salt Fest which often includes a luncheon, baking contests, a classic car show, live music, and a talent show. To find out about this year's Salt Fest visit the official website for details.

Plan your trip to the Salt Palace and Salt Fest
Website: saltfest.net
Address: 100 W Garland St, Grand Saline, TX 75140

HAWKINS

Pancake Capital and Birthplace of "Aunt Jemima"

In 1995, the Texas State Legislature deemed Hawkins the "Pancake Capital of Texas." This is not because of any special recipe or restaurant, but due to the fact that Hawkins is the birthplace of Lillian Richard, the woman who portrayed Aunt Jemima for the Quaker Oats Company for 37 years.

Upon retiring, Lillian Richard returned to her hometown, where she lived out the rest of her life. She passed away in 1956 and her body rests in Fouke Memorial Cemetery. In 2012, a Texas State Historical Marker was erected in her honor.

Beauty and the Book

Beauty and the Book is a beauty salon/bookstore owned and operated by the vivacious cosmetologist and entrepreneur, Kathy L. Murphy (formerly Patrick.) Beauty and the Book was Murphy's "lemons to lemonade" response to losing her job as a book sales representative in 1999. Shortly after opening the shop over in Jefferson, Murphy created the Pulpwood Queens and Timber Guys book club, a franchise that now has over 550 chapters and around 3,000 members worldwide.

Murphy and her book club have been featured on everything from *Newsweek*, *Time* magazine, *The Wall Street Journal*, *Los Angeles Times*, "The Oprah Winfrey Show!," and "Good Morning, America." As with her salon/bookstore, the main objective of the club is to have fun. The club's motto is, "Where tiaras are mandatory and reading good books is the RULE!"

A few years ago, Murphy also launched an annual festival for book club members called the Pulpwood Queens Girlfriend Weekend, which draws 400 to 500 men and women to Jefferson, Texas each January. Keynote speakers at this event have included Fannie Flagg, Pat Conroy, Carol Alt, and more.

As of 2014, Murphy's Beauty and the Book has moved from Jefferson to Hawkins, Texas. It's currently in with The Nail and Hair Shed, so before you plan your trip, double check her website to get the most up-to-date information.

Plan your trip to Beauty & the Book/Nail & Hair Shed
Websites: beautyandthebook.com pulpwoodqueen.com and beautyandthebookshow.com
Address: 2501 B S. FM 2869, Hawkins, Texas 75765

JACKSBORO

Overview of Jacksboro, Texas

There's not a lot going on in Jacksboro, but it is lucky; unlike so many other small towns, the main highway takes drivers right through its historic town square. If Jacksboro can hang in there, it could blossom into something really special. I wouldn't suggest it as a primary destination, but if you happen to pass by, there are a few things worth checking out.

Jacksboro Town Square

Although historic, the current courthouse is rather bland compared to others in Texas. While its 1940 modern style design was surely quite thrilling in its day, I find it boxy and plain in comparison to buildings erected during Texas' Golden Era of Courthouses (1880 - 1900.)

Plan your trip to Jacksboro Town Square
Address: 100 N Main St # 208, Jacksboro, TX 76458

Old Fashioned Soda Fountain

My favorite discovery in Jacksboro is City Drug, a family-owned business on the south side of the square. Besides having an old fashioned soda fountain where you can order patty-melts and chocolate malts, City Drug is a fully up-to-date compounding pharmacy with delivery service, 24-Hour Emergency service, and a drive-thru window. The soda fountain dates back to at least 1911, and is one of the few left in Texas. They also sell office supplies, knick knacks, and cosmetics. The drug store is managed by a father-son team, both registered pharmacists. Ralph Hammond has owned City Drug since 1960 and his son, Rod, is now his partner.

Plan your trip to City Drug
Website: citydrug-jacksboro.com
Address: 104 East Belknap St., Jacksboro, TX 76458

The Main Street Bistro and B&B

Another Jacksboro gem is the Main Street Bistro and B&B which is housed in a beautifully restored stone building across from the courthouse. The ground floor houses a Starbucks, which is the "bistro" part of the equation. Behind the building, you find a well-landscaped courtyard which includes a bandstand and a fountain surrounded by flowers. Follow the extra wide staircase (to allow for hoopskirts, perhaps?) upstairs to visit the sitting area and guest rooms, which are elegantly decorated and very cozy.

Plan your trip to the Main Street Bistro and B&B
Website: mainstreetbedandbreakfast.com
Address: 119 N Main St, Jacksboro, TX 76458

Fort Richardson State Park

From 1867 to 1878, Fort Richardson was a US Army installation a mile south of Jacksboro. Texas had several such installations at that time, a series of forts meant to encourage white folks to settle in north central and west Texas.

If history interests you, take a guided tour with one of the park rangers who will show you through the fort's historic structures, which include a bakery, morgue, commissary, hospital and powder magazine. Replicas of the officer's and enlisted men's barracks are also part of the tour. I'm not sure if all the guides are as much fun as Ray, but that's who showed us around when my husband and I visited. He was casual and humorous, but also very informative.

Other activities here include camping, biking, hiking, horseback trails (b.y.o. horse) and picnics. Plus, the fort's Quarry Lake is periodically stocked with bass, trout, and catfish for those who like to fish.

Fort Richardson also hosts special events throughout the year, such as living history presentations, a barbecue cook-off, fishing tournaments, and military reenactments. Check out their online events calendar to plan your visit.

Plan your trip to Fort Richardson State Park
Website: tpwd.state.tx.us/state-parks/fort-richardson
Address: 228 State Park Road 61, Jacksboro, TX 76458

JEFFERSON

Overview of Jefferson, Texas

With its brick streets, horse drawn carriages, wrought iron railings, and abundance of Greek revival architecture, a visit to Jefferson, Texas can make you feel like you've stepped onto a movie set for New Orleans in the late 1800's.

This town's resemblance to the "Big Easy" is no mere affectation, but a genuine part of its heritage. Jefferson has so much in common with New Orleans, including brick streets, carriage rides, and wrought iron rail that it's sometimes called the "Little Easy."

While it's a small town now, from 1845 to 1872 Jefferson was a major Texas port, second only to the port of Galveston. Steamboats laden with cotton and other goods powered upriver all the way from New Orleans, thereby earning Jefferson the nickname, "Riverport to the Southwest." Shortly after the Civil War, Jefferson was the sixth largest city in Texas with a population of 30,000.

In 1873, the Army Corps of Engineers used explosives to remove a huge raft of logs downstream from Jefferson. As a result, the water level in the bayou dropped so much that big steamboats were unable to make it to town. At the same time, transportation by railway was becoming the norm, and before long, Jefferson's life as a major Texas port came to an end.

Although the population has shrunk to a mere 2,000, this tiny town is still bustling. At any given time there are between 50 to 80 bed and breakfast inns operating to keep up with the demand for lodging. Every year, Jefferson plays host to a variety of festivals and community events, including a historic homes tour, the Diamond Bessie Murder Trial reenactment, the Texas Bigfoot Conference, an antique car show, the Pulpwood Queen's Girlfriend Fest, and much more. Even if you just pop in for a day trip when no festivals are happening, there is still plenty to see and do in this unique little town.

Mardi Gras Upriver

Hotels and B&B's are often booked a year in advance for Jefferson's Mardi Gras, so don't plan a spur of the moment trip during this time. Known as "Mardi Gras Upriver" this annual celebration kicks off with the Queen

Mab Ball, and is followed by parades (including a children's parade), King Cake, beads, masked revelers, and live music. Jefferson celebrated its first Mardi Gras in 1871, so it has lots of traditions.

Turning Basin Riverboat Tours the Big Cypress Bayou

At $8 per person, the hour-long riverboat cruise down Big Cypress Bayou in Jefferson, Texas is well worth it. The boat captain is entertaining, the setting is beautiful, and shutterbugs will be in photo-heaven.

Our boat was captained by John Nance, who kept us entertained with a mixture of historical information, local lore, and facts about nature. After showing us a photo of a huge snapping turtle, John told us how a high school buddy of his earned the name "Stumpy" after having several fingers bitten off by just such a creature while noodling for catfish. (In case you don't know, "noodling" is the term for catching fish by hand. Pretty crazy activity to do in snapping turtle country.)

Plan your trip to Turning Basin Riverboat Tours
Website: jeffersonbayoutours.com
Address: 200 Bayou St., Jefferson, TX 75657

Diamond Bessie Murder Trial Reenactment

Annie Stone was a flamboyant young prostitute who earned the nickname "Diamond Bessie" thanks to the flashy jewelry she wore everywhere she went. She was last seen alive on January 21, 1877 crossing the bayou with her lover, Abraham Rothschild, as the two went for a picnic. A few hours later, Rothschild was seen crossing the bridge back to Jefferson, alone. When folks asked where Bessie was, he claimed she had decided to stay with some friends across the river.

The next morning, however, locals spotted Rothschild wearing Diamond Bessie's rings as he ate breakfast at a hotel. Afterwards, he boarded a train to Cincinnati, but people thought it odd that he used Bessie's luggage to carry his belongings.

On February 5, 1877 Bessie's body was discovered in the woods with remnants from a picnic lunch scattered around her. She had been shot once in the head, and wore no jewelry. Meanwhile, in Ohio, a distraught Rothschild tried to kill himself, but merely succeeded in shooting his right eye out. After spending a few days in the hospital, he was extradited to Texas, where he stood trial for Diamond Bessie's demise.

Since Abraham Rothschild came from a wealthy, high society family, and Bessie was a lowly prostitute, the case gained a lot of attention. If it were today, Nancy Grace would be all over it.

Although Rothschild was never found guilty of murder, and quietly faded into obscurity, Diamond Bessie became a figure of folklore. Every year in Jefferson during its annual Pilgrimage Festival, a play entitled The Diamond Bessie Murder Trial, featuring dialogue derived directly from court transcripts, is performed. Diamond Bessie's grave in Jefferson's Oakwood Cemetery is a popular tourist attraction. Although it remained unmarked for years, it now bears a tombstone reputedly installed in the night by an unknown admirer.

Plan your trip to Diamond Bessie's Grave
Website: jeffersoncemeterytour.org
Address: Old Oakwood Cemetery, 607 N Alley St Jefferson, TX 75657

Plan your trip to Diamond Bessie Murder Trial Reenactment
Website: visitjeffersontexas.com/calendar.cfm

Steven Spielberg's Ghostly Encounter

The Excelsior House is the oldest hotel in East Texas, and has been in operation since the 1850's. Over the years, several prestigious guests have spent the night there including Oscar Wilde, Ulysses S. Grant, Rutherford B. Hayes, and Lady Bird Johnson. I would add the famous director Steven Spielberg to this list except for one small detail. Rather than spend an entire night, Mr. Spielberg scurried off in the wee hours claiming that he was being pestered by ghosts.

Although the current hotel manager refuses to discuss the paranormal, Steven Spielberg is on the record with the *Dallas Morning News* regarding this incident. In subsequent interviews over the years, he has even referred to the Excelsior House as one of two haunted hotels he has stayed in (the other being the Stanley Hotel in Colorado upon which Stephen King based the hotel in his book *The Shining*.)

The incident Spielberg described to the *Dallas Morning News* took place in the 1970's while he was scouting locations for the movie "Sugarland Express." After a long day, he retired to his room and tossed his briefcase onto a rocking chair. According to Spielberg, the chair immediately tossed the briefcase back at him. Chalking it up to the overstuffed pillow, Spielberg shrugged the incident off

132

and tried to get some sleep. Sometime around midnight, however, he awoke to find a little boy standing by the bed. Before he could make sense of this, the boy asked if he was ready for breakfast. That's when Mr. Spielberg leapt from bed, gathered up his film crew, and at 2:00 a.m. made them drive over to the town of Marshall to find a different hotel.

Shortly after this incident, Spielberg wrote and produced the movie "Poltergeist," leading many to believe that his stay at the Excelsior Hotel provided inspiration for that paranormal movie. In case you are wondering, Steven Spielberg stayed in the Jay Gould room, which is considered by those in the know to be the most haunted room in the hotel.

Plan your trip to the Excelsior House Hotel
Website: theexcelsiorhouse.com
Address: 211 W. Austin, Jefferson, TX 75657

Historic Jefferson Ghost Walk

If you are wondering why the SyFy, Travel and Discover channels all describe Jefferson as the "most haunted small town in Texas," consider taking the Historical Jefferson Texas Ghost Tour to see for yourself.

Led by local historian and self-described skeptic, Jodi Breckenridge, this walking tour takes you by several haunted locations in the historic downtown. Each trip is different, but Breckenridge strives to take participants inside at least one paranormal hot spot on every tour.

Tours last a good 90 minutes and are a great way to stretch your legs after a big meal. The night I attended, there was a crowd of 75+ people.

I must confess that no orbs appeared in the photos I took, nor did our group experience anything anomalous. I was surprised, however, at how many people in the tour were repeat customers. Several of them had eerie tales to share about things they experienced on previous excursions with Breckenridge.

My husband doesn't believe in anything the slightest bit woo-woo, but he thoroughly enjoyed the ghost tour. He described it as an entertaining after-hours tour of historic downtown Jefferson, and I must agree. Still, the next time I go (and there will be a next time), I hope to see a ghost.

Plan your trip to the Historic Jefferson Ghost Walk
Website: jeffersonghostwalk.com
Address: Corner of Austin and Vale Streets, Jefferson, TX 75657

The Grove

If Jefferson is such a haunted town, then it should be no surprise that there is more than one ghost tour available. Not only did several people on the tour insist that The Grove is a must-see, but as of this writing, it rates as the number one tourist attraction in Jefferson, Texas on TripAdvisor. It has been featured on numerous TV shows, including "William Shatner's Weird or What?" "If Walls Could Talk," and "Penn & Teller: Bullshit!" as well as being named "one of the top 12 most haunted houses in America" by "This Old House."

There are a couple of major differences between The Grove and most other paranormal tours. First of all, The Grove concentrates on a single dwelling, the Stilley-Young House which was built in 1861 and is a Recorded Texas Historic Landmark that is also on the National Register of Historic Places. Secondly, tours of The Grove take place during daylight hours, rather than after dark. This increases your chance of taking ghostly photos because you won't have to use a flash. Also, if like me, your spouse doesn't believe in ghosts, The Grove is a lovely tour of a historic home.

Unfortunately, we weren't able to book a tour with The Grove during our visit to Jefferson, so I cannot report on it firsthand. It comes so highly recommended from other sources, however, that I am including it here, anyway. If you take the tour, let me know what you think.

Plan your trip The Grove
Website: thegrove-jefferson.com
Address: 405 Moseley St, Jefferson, TX 75657

Scarlet O'Hardy's Gone with the Wind Museum

My heart was set on visiting Scarlet O'Hardy's Gone with the Wind Museum, so I was disappointed to learn that this venue is no longer in operation. Perhaps someone will take the reigns and revive this place. After all, tomorrow is another day!

Museum of Measurement and Time

While wandering around town (a delightful activity in Jefferson, Texas) I discovered the Museum of Measurement and Time which showcases an assortment of time-keeping and landscaping devices. This quirky little museum also includes a large collection of salt and pepper shakers, for some reason.

Plan your trip to the Museum of Measurement and Time
Address: 301 N. Polk, Jefferson, TX 75657

East Texas Bigfoot Sightings

Whether you call them Sasquatch, Bigfoot, or wood apes, the piney woods of east Texas are a hot spot for sightings of big, hairy creatures. If nothing else, this undocumented hominid has captured the local imagination to the extent that several monster movies have been filmed nearby including the "Creature from Black Lake," "Legend of Boggy Creek," and most recently east Texas' answer to "Sharknado," entitled "Bigfoot Wars."

While Jefferson has hosted several Bigfoot Conferences, there is no set location for this annual event, so keep your eye on the North American Wood ape Conservancy (NAWAC) website for details.

For more information on East Texas Bigfoot Sightings
Website: woodape.org

Historic Jefferson Railways

This cute little N gauge train takes passengers on a 40-minute, narrated tour through the Piney Woods and alongside the Big Cypress Bayou. The train was originally used in the Six Guns amusement park in Florida, which is why the passenger car doors display a logo featuring a pair of crossed six-shooters on them. The ride is a fun way to get a feel for the area, and the open-air passenger cars are comfortable even on a hot summer day.

Plan your trip to Historic Jefferson Railways
Website: jeffersonrailway.com
Address: 400 East Austin, Jefferson, TX 75657

Carnegie Library

Out of 34 libraries built in Texas using money donated by the Scottish-American philanthropist Andrew Carnegie, Jefferson's is one of four in the state that still operates as a public library.

The building, which dates from 1907, features a cheery yellow paint job, tall white pillars, and like so many historic buildings in this town, it is well-maintained. Just because it's old, doesn't mean it's not up-to-date. The library offers free internet and, on the day I visited, the librarians were friendly. Walk upstairs and you will find a large ballroom that serves many functions, from hosting club meetings and classes, to an annual New Year's Eve ball.

Plan your trip to the Carnegie Library
Website: jeffersoncarnegielibrary.com
Address: 301 W. Lafayette, Jefferson, TX 75657

Jay Gould Railroad Car

Built in 1888, Jay Gould's personal railroad car was the height of technology and luxury for its day. Built to his specifications, it contains a lounge, four staterooms, a kitchen, a dining room, a butler pantry, and a bathroom. It is now on display in Jefferson, Texas as tribute to an alleged feud between Mr. Gould and the town's citizens. While there is probably more legend than truth to this squabble, it makes for a good story.

In the late 1800's, Jay Gould allegedly proposed bringing one of his railways to Jefferson. Not only did he suggest laying the track right down the middle of Main Street, but he wanted the city of Jefferson to pay for this privilege.

Locals took offense to Gould's stingy demands and let him know they didn't need no stinking railroad because they had steamboats coming up from New Orleans all the time.

Gould was so enraged by the city of Jefferson's disregard for what he considered a great opportunity that he tacked an angry message onto his signature in the Excelsior House Hotel's guest registry which ominously reads, "The end of Jefferson."

Whether this tale is true or not, history has proven Jay Gould right. In 1873, when steamboats quit coming to town, the economy dwindled and Jefferson's boomtown days were over. On the other hand, if the railroad had come to town, the "progress" and economic growth it would have brought would most likely have wiped out all the historic buildings and charming architecture that grace the town today.

In any case, the city of Jefferson purchased Mr. Gould's personal railway car in 1954. It now sits across from the Excelsior House Hotel, which is where you should inquire if you would like a personal tour.

Plan your trip to the Jay Gould Railway Car
Address: W. Austin St, Jefferson, TX 75657

Lone Star Carriage Company

One of my favorite things about Jefferson is that it is such a walkable town, a rare quality in Texas. That said, there are times when nothing beats a horse (or mule) drawn carriage ride.

The Lone Star Carriage Company offers three different kinds of rides. If you feel like learning, take the 30-minute narrated historic tour. If you feel like romance, ask for the 30-minute scenic tour without narration. For a little of both, opt for their hour-long trip which takes you on a wider circuit through Jefferson and combines scenery with history.

For an impromptu trip Thursday - Saturday, look for the carriages at the corner of Austin and Market Streets in downtown Jefferson.

Plan your trip to the Lone Star Carriage Company
Website: jeffersontexascarriage.com
Address: 222 West Austin Street, Jefferson, TX 75657

Jefferson General Store

Yes, it's a store, but it's a fun, old-fashioned store, much like the "five and dimes" that were once a common feature across America.

I enjoyed every inch of the Jefferson General Store, from the bar stools along its soda fountain to its creaky wood plank floors. The store carries everything from homemade pickles and jams, to toys, hats, games, clothing, kitchen wares and more. The vast candy selection includes a wide variety of long-forgotten brands in vintage style wrappers, to barrels of saltwater taffy and strange new candies, of which I had never heard. The Jefferson General Store also sells ice cream in waffle cones made on-site, and as of this writing a cup of fresh coffee still goes for a nickel per cup.

Plan your trip to the Jefferson General Store
Website: jeffersongeneralstore.com
Address: 113 E. Austin St. Jefferson, Texas 75657

MINEOLA

Overview of Mineola, Texas

It's unclear exactly how the town of Mineola got its name. While some claim a railway official named it after his daughter, Ola, and her BFF, Minnie, others say the name was created by a surveyor who combined his daughter's name with her friend, Minna. Either way, Mineola has a much nicer ring to it than Sodom, which is what the town was originally called.

In 1873, the International-Great Northern (IGN) and the Texas and Pacific railroad raced each other to see which line could reach Mineola first. The IGN squeaked into town a mere 15 minutes before its rival. The town incorporated in 1877, and despite a devastating fire, it soon became a bustling little burg full of churches, hotels, banks and several schools.

Located at the junction of US highways 80 and 69, Mineola is situated in Wood County which, true to its name, is a highly-forested section of the East Texas Piney Woods.

Early industries included lumber, farming, and a chair factory, although things really got hopping once a railroad terminal was added and oil was discovered nearby. Texas tea, y'all!

These days, Mineola is a peaceful little community with a population of 4,515 as of the 2010 US census. In springtime, the roads are lined with bluebonnets and other wildflowers. In autumn, it's perfect for leaf-peeping, Texas style. This makes the region ideal for scenic drives, with impromptu produce stands and garage sales a common sight on your way in and out of town.

Amtrak Station in Mineola

In its heyday, Mineola was a terminal for train crews and featured two railroad hotels, one on either side of the tracks. The railroad is still a big part of this city, which is one of the few small towns in Texas to have an Amtrak station. Since Mineola's main sights are within walking distance of the train depot, and there are daily stops from both Dallas and Forth Worth, a car-less weekend getaway is a viable option.

Plan your trip to the Amtrak Station in Mineola
Website: amtrak.com
Address: 115 East Front Street, Mineola, TX 75773

Historic Downtown Mineola

Thanks to its designations as a Texas Main Street City since 1989 and a National Main Street City since 2000, Mineola has done a good job preserving its historic buildings. The downtown is still paved with bright red bricks, and the streets are lined with specialty shops, restaurants, and top-notch antiquing. Many alleyways have faded advertisements painted on them, as well as murals painted more recently. Mineola's historic downtown is full of mom and pop shops, and has several worthwhile antique stores to explore.

Mineola Historical Museum

Located just one block from Mineola's main street, this free museum if staffed by enthusiastic historians. If you have a question about Mineola, or just Texas, in general, they are more than willing to help out.

Plan your trip to the Mineola Historical Museum
Website: mincolahistoricalmuseum.com
Address: 114 N Pacific, Mineola, TX 75773

Lake Country Playhouse

Lake Country Playhouse is one of the longest running movie theaters in Texas, having been in operation since 1920. Despite its old-school looks and retro neon sign, this

145

cinema plays first-run movies, community theater productions and even becomes a haunted house called "Warehouse of Terror" in October.

Plan your trip to the Lake Country Playhouse
Website: lakecountryplayhouse.com
Address: 114 N Johnson St, Mineola, TX 75773

Live Music on the Streets of Mineola

Every Saturday morning, acoustic musicians are invited to head downtown, stand in a shady doorway or street corner and play solo or with friends. I saw several guitarists picking and a-grinning during my visit.

Mineola Farmers Market

There is a small farmers market at the train depot in downtown Mineola every Saturday starting in May and continuing for as long as the weather holds (most likely July or August.)

Birthplace of Miss Ima Hogg

While Mineola has many Texas State Historical markers, the quirkiest one I ran across is at 125 N. Line Street, where a plaque stands in front of the house where Ima

Hogg was born on July 10, 1882. If you think "North West" is an odd name, imagine going through life as "Ima Hogg."

While rumors of a twin sister named Ura have persisted, Ima was the only daughter of Jim Hogg, who later became governor of the state of Texas. Why he named her Ima is a matter of much debate, but Miss Hogg's life was no joke. She never married, but devoted her life to art and philanthropy instead.

Plan your trip to the Birthplace of Miss Ima Hogg
Address: 125 N. Line Street, Mineola, TX 75773

Mineola Nature Preserve

Whether you feel like hiking, biking, walking, camping, birding, fishing, picnicking, or riding your horse, the Mineola Nature Preserve can help you. With 2,911 acres of nature to explore, including a beehive you can view through safety glass, this gorgeous public park is open daily to give you the nature-fix you crave. They even offer stargazing parties and other educational activities.

Plan your trip to the Mineola Nature Preserve
Website: mineolanaturepreserve.com
Address: 1860 County Road 2724, Mineola, TX 75773

Blueberry Ridge Farm

The oldest certified organic blueberry farm in Texas is a short drive to the east of Mineola. During blueberry season, it's a U-pick destination. It also has a country store called, oddly enough, "Country Store," where they sell blueberry-related items, molasses, local honey, old-fashioned candy, goats milk soap and other items you might expect at a, well, country store.

Plan your trip to the Blueberry Ridge Farm
Website: blueberryridgefarm.com
Address: 2785 U.S. 80, Mineola, TX 75773

Kitchen's Hardware

If you're a fan of the "Gilmore Girls" TV show, then a restaurant in an old hardware store is not an odd concept to you. If not, get used to it, because Kitchen's Hardware is here to stay. My husband and I dined here on the recommendation of our B&B hosts at the Munzesheimer Manor, and they did not steer us wrong. I ordered the peppered steak, and I've never had beef that tender in my life. The setting is a lot of fun, too. It's like a hardware store museum, with its pot bellied stove, a hand-operated Otis rope elevator, and other items from yesteryear everywhere you look.

Plan your trip to Kitchen's Hardware
Address: 119 E Broad St, Mineola, TX 75773

East Texas Burger Company

With its sassy wait staff and tasty food (gotta love those sweet potato fries!), the East Texas Burger Company is a good choice and easy on the wallet. I got a kick from all the napkin doodles and notes tacked to the wall. They're fun to read while waiting for your order to come up. Legend has it that Bonnie and Clyde once dined at this burger joint. Other famous clientele includes Dan Rather and Sissy Spacek.

Plan your trip to East Texas Burger Company
Website: easttexasburger.com
Address: 126 E Broad St, Mineola, TX 75773

Munzesheimer Manor

Munzesheimer Manor is a consistently award-winning bed and breakfast, as voted by *Inn Traveler* magazine, the *Dallas Morning News*, *Arrington's B&B Journal* and more. But really, all accolades aside, this lovely B&B makes a wonderful getaway from the hustle and bustle of daily life.

Talk about a home away from home! Munzesheimer Manor offers rooms in a beautifully restored Victorian home as well as accommodations in adjacent cottages. My husband

and I stayed in the railroad-themed Engineer's room and we loved it.

Full disclosure here: When I'm traveling on a research trip, it can be very "rush-rush" but the innkeepers, Bob and Sherry Murray, made us feel so welcome that I really just wanted to toss all my notes to the side and kick back for a couple of days. In fact, Munzesheimer Manor is so wonderful that my husband has requested that I book us there again as proper guests rather than travel researchers.

Plan your trip to Munzesheimer Manor
Website: munzesheimer.com
Address: 202 N Newsom St, Mineola, TX 75773

MINERAL WELLS

Overview of Mineral Wells

In the 1880's Judge James Alvis Lynch and his wife, Armenia, moved to north Texas and dug a well. Since the water tasted strange, they let only their livestock drink it. After seeing how well their animals thrived, the pair began drinking the water, too. That's when things got interesting.

You see, James had stomach problems and Armenia suffered from rheumatism. Once they began drinking the well water, the couple's health conditions promptly cleared up. In fact, the whole family, including all nine children, felt better after drinking the strange-tasting water.

As word spread of the Lynch's healing water, people came from all around to try it. Many stayed, which is how the town of Mineral Wells got its start.

Not only did the water make the Lynch's healthy, but it made them wealthy, too. Judge Lynch sold the water for a dime per cup, which is more than a whole loaf of bread cost at the time. He even became the town's first mayor.

Famous Water Company of Mineral Wells, Texas

In the early 1900's, a young pharmacist named Ed Dismuke came to Mineral Wells. Dismuke had nothing to lose; doctors down in Waco said he would be dead within a year due to an untreatable stomach condition.

Dismuke not only felt better after drinking the local healing water, but he lived to be 92. He was such a believer in the healing powers of the local wells that he opened the Famous Water Company in 1904 so he could bottle and sell the stuff.

The water of Mineral Wells has had many nicknames through the years, but one that stuck is "crazy water." Details are fuzzy, but apparently a woman who suffered from some sort of mental illness was allegedly cured after drinking water from Mineral Wells.

Crazy Water Renaissance

In the 1990's a couple named Carol and Mike Elder bought the Famous Water Company and set about reviving its healthy reputation. (If you can't find it at your local grocery, you can buy it online.)

Just what does this unusual water contain? According to regulators, Crazy Water contains magnesium, potassium, calcium, silica, and trace amounts of lithium. If you visit the official website, it lists the exact ratios of minerals in the water. Crazy Water is even endorsed by hockey players, cyclists, and other athletes.

As of late 2013, the Famous Water Company offers mineral baths to the public. Now you can experience the healing benefits of Crazy Water by soaking in it. I have yet to bathe in Crazy Water, but it is high on my Texas to-do list.

Plan your trip to the Famous Water Company
Website: drinkcrazywater.com
Address: 209 N. W. 6th Street, Mineral Wells, Texas 76067

The Baker Hotel

At 14 stories tall, the Baker Hotel of Mineral Wells was the first skyscraper erected outside a major metropolitan area. Although it opened to the public shortly after the stock market crash of 1929, the Baker Hotel thrived, attracting rich and famous clientele such as Roy Rogers, Clark Gable, Lawrence Welk, Marlene Dietrich, Will Rogers, Helen Keller, Judy Garland, Glenn Miller, and the Three Stooges.

It's rumored that Bonnie and Clyde were such frequent guests that special accommodations were made for the pair, such as placing them in a room near an outside exit, and removing the carpet in front of their door so they could hear approaching footsteps.

You may be wondering what drew people to a hotel in the middle of nowhere? The Baker Hotel featured many newfangled luxuries for its time, such as an Olympic-sized pool filled with water from the local mineral wells, and ice water circulated to all 450 of its guest rooms. Its facilities included an on-site beauty salon, a gymnasium, bowling alley, and meeting rooms to accommodate 2,500 guests. Hotel keys controlled the lights and fans in each room so that when a guest left, these would be automatically turn off. To top it off, the Baker Hotel was fully air-conditioned, something completely unheard of back then.

After World War II, business began to decline. Even so, the Baker Hotel hosted three major political conventions in the 1950's (two for the Texas Republican Party and one for the Texas Democratic Party.) Business worsened in the 1960's and the hotel sputtered to a full stop in 1972, when the doors were closed for good.

The mammoth building was still used for special occasions, and was still in good enough shape to host a high school prom as recently as 1996. Sadly, it has since been vandalized and now has a leaky roof, broken windows, peeling paint, and damaged plaster throughout. In 1982, the hotel was placed on the National Historic Register, but it will take a lot of effort to restore this once-magnificent building to its former glory.

With such a storied past, is it any surprise that some folks claim that the Baker Hotel is haunted? Local paranormal groups as well as television shows such as "Ghost Adventures" have held investigations there.

While the Baker Hotel is boarded up and closed to the public, it's worth stopping by and snapping a few photos from the outside.

Plan your trip to the Baker Hotel
Website: bakerhotel.us
Address: 200 East Hubbard St, Mineral Wells, Texas 76067

OLNEY

In 1972, while hanging out at the local drugstore, Olney residents, Jack Northrup and Jack Bishop, decided to have a little fun with strangers seated nearby who were obviously eavesdropping on them. I should add that around the town of Olney, Northrup and Bishop are known as the "One Armed Jacks" since both men are missing upper-limbs.

The two Jacks began describing how much they enjoy hunting with bolt-action rifles and muzzle-loaded shotguns. Although they kept straight faces, this was a joke; it's impossible to shoot either of those guns with only one arm.

What started as a bit of mischief has grown into an annual tradition in Olney, Texas. Every September, the city hosts its One Arm Dove Hunt. This two-day festival includes events such as a one-armed skeet shoot, a one-armed horseshoe tossing, a one-arm cow-chip tossing, and a "10 cents per finger" breakfast. And, yes, there actually is a dove hunt, although the hunting contests are beside the point. The main purpose of this unique festival is to provide fun and fellowship for men, women, and children who are missing upper-limbs.

Plan your trip to the One Arm Dove Hunt
Website: http://www.onearmdovehunt.com/

PARIS

Overview of Paris

Paris Texas makes a fun day trip. While several Texan towns share names with European cities: London, Athens and Dublin to name a few, what makes Paris so special is how the town plays up its French name, riffing on it like a jazz theme.

Eiffel Tower Replica

For example, the Eiffel Tower replica built in the early 90's with donated parts and volunteer labor by a local factory, Babcock and Wilcox Co. Unlike other replicas around the USA, Paris chose to add a touch of "yee haw" to their "ooh-la-la" by topping their Eiffel Tower with a bright red cowboy hat.

At 65 feet high, the replica is pretty teeny compared to the original Eiffel Tower in that *other* Paris, and it looks a lot like an oil derrick. Still, it's much taller than anything nearby and is mighty photogenic.

Plan your trip to the Eiffel Tower Replica
Address: Love Civic Center, 2025 South Collegiate Drive, Paris, TX 75460

Historic Downtown Paris

After taking some photos of the Eiffel Tower replica, set your GPS for downtown, and get ready to do some walking. The citizens of Paris have kept their little city in good shape. A gorgeous marble fountain stands in the center of the historical downtown, creating a lovely centerpiece for all the mom and pop stores surrounding it.

Paris makes a good Texas day trip for antique lovers. Nearly every store downtown offers a free map listing at least 15 different antique shops within walking distance of town square. There is also a year-round farmer's market near downtown where you can enjoy what local growers have to offer.

Plan your trip to Historic Downtown Paris
Address: Paris Texas Chamber of Commerce, 8 West Plaza, Paris, TX 75460

Historic Neighborhoods and Architecture

Downtown Paris, Texas features older buildings with interesting details, such as gargoyles and mosaic tiles. Don't miss the Lamar County Courthouse, a pink granite structure decorated with intricately carved columns, smug-faced lions and other striking details.

The Historic Neighborhood of Paris, Texas is worth driving through to check out all the lovely Victorian homes and wonderful old trees. One of these historic homes, the Sam Bell Maxey House, is now a museum, although as of this writing, it is closed for remodeling.

Plan your trip to the Sam Bell Maxey House
Website: visitsambellmaxeyhouse.com
Address: 812 S Church St, Paris, TX 75460

Jesus in Cowboy Boots

No day trip to Paris, Texas is complete without a visit to Evergreen Cemetery, where you can see a statue depicting Jesus wearing a pair of cowboy boots.

Tales abound regarding the Jesus in Cowboy Boots, which stands atop the grave of a fellow named Willet Babcock. Some say it isn't even supposed to be Jesus, but an angel, instead. Another rumor claims that the sculptor was bad at depicting feet, so he chose cowboy boots to avoid the anatomical challenge.

This statue is actually the 20-foot tall grave marker honoring a man named Willet Babcock, who died in 1888.

While impressive, it would hardly be the quirky tourist attraction that it has become were it not for the unusual footwear worn by the cross-bearing figure it depicts; instead of the bare feet or sandals one often associates with Biblical folk, this one wears cowboy boots.

Who was Willet Babcock?

Willet Babcock was a Civil War veteran who moved from Ithaca, New York to Paris, Texas where he became a prominent businessman with an interest in art and theater. Mr. Babcock's love of the arts is evidenced by the fact that his furniture showroom in downtown Paris also housed the local opera house on its second floor.

Babcock commissioned his impressive headstone from the Paris Marble Works in 1880, 8 years before he was laid to rest on the south side of town in Evergreen Cemetery.

There's argument over whether the statue depicts Jesus carrying a cross, or whether it's actually supposed to be a mourning angel leaning against a cross. Some folks claim the face is too feminine looking to be Jesus. While I could tell that he or she did not wear a beard, I couldn't decide for myself whether the face was masculine or feminine, since the statue was heavily backlit during my visit. Next time I go, I will try to get a better look.

Mysteries Surround Jesus in Cowboy Boots

More rumors surround the statue, as well. For one thing, unlike most of the other 40,000 graves in Evergreen Cemetery, Babcock's faces towards the west instead of the east.

This might not seem like a big deal in our day and age; everyone has a GPS now, right? Seriously though, back in the 1800's, the direction your body was laid to rest mattered to people. Facing west was weird because it breaks with the old Christian tradition of burying people facing east (so they will be facing the right direction when Jesus returns to earth.)

Modern viewers have also been taken aback by the upside down torches engraved on the base of the monument. Some have even interpreted the torches and the monument direction to mean that Mr. Babcock and his wife were atheists. While I am also puzzled by the direction the Babcock monument faces, I do know that inverted torches are a Christian symbol

What Do Upside Down Torches Mean on a Grave?

So, what is the significance of upside down torches on a headstone? You know how a candle will go out if you hold it upside down? An inverted torch symbolizes the idea that one's life is like a flame, and that even when this flame is extinguished by death, one's soul continues to burn in the afterlife.

Whatever the case may be, if you enjoy traipsing through old graveyards, Evergreen Cemetery is a real treat. Not only is it big, but it's been around since 1866, and is full of well-crafted grave markers, as well as lots of big old trees.

Plan your visit to Evergreen Cemetery
Address: 560 Evergreen St, Paris, TX 75460

Trail de Paris Solar System Replica

The Trail de Paris is a well-maintained public path for walking, jogging, and cycling. Not only is this lovely trail heavily-wooded, but the Valley of the Caddo Star Gazer's Club recently created a scale model of the solar system along the way.

On the day of my visit, it was too hot to walk the whole trail, but I made it to Jupiter, which is 4 inches in diameter. Elsewhere, they have the sun at 42 inches round and, yes, they include Pluto, even though it is a mere 0.07 inch in diameter at this scale.

Plan your trip to the Trail de Paris
Address: Noyes Stadium, 1245 24th Street, Paris, TX 75460

Famous Campbell Soup Can

While researching Paris, Texas, I kept reading about an allegedly "huge" can of tomato soup on display in Paris. While it's true that the entrance sign for the local Campbell's Soup factory does feature a big can of soup, I wouldn't quite call it, "huge." Still, it is worthy of a drive-by photo, especially if you are an Andy Warhol fan.

Plan your trip to the Campbell Soup Can
Address: Campbell Soup Factory, 500 NW Loop 286 Paris, TX 75460

RICHARDSON

Pegasus Theatre's Living Black and White™ Play

Every January, Pegasus Theatre presents a unique production at the Eisemann Center in Richardson, Texas: a play that looks and feels like an old black and white movie. Through special trademarked make-up techniques, carefully chosen costuming, clever lighting, and stylized acting, the experience is so good that when a woman in a bright red dress steps onto the stage after the curtain call, it's jarring to the eyes. Even my camera struggled to make sense of that moment; she came out looking splotchy and yellow in a few shots.

A Parody of Film Noir & Crime Fiction

These Living Black & White™ productions are the brainchild of Pegasus Theatre founder and Artistic Director Kurt Kleinmann, who also stars in the shows as Harry Hunsacker. The plays are set in the 1930's and 40's and feature the detective/aspiring actor, Harry Hunsacker, and his paid-by-the-hour assistant and pal, Nigel Grouse. The stories are a parody of film noir and hard boiled detective movies. While Kleinmann's main characters were inspired by Sherlock Holmes and Dr. Watson, he adds a comedic twist by making the detective dim-witted while the assistant is the clever one.

Rehearsal for Murder!

The Living Black & White™ show I saw is entitled "Rehearsal for Murder!" and is set in the year 1946. The story centers on a cop named Lt. Foster who is excited to escape the big city after inheriting a hotel in the Green Mountains of Vermont. Before he can kick back and enjoy the good life, Lt. Foster discovers that the leading man for a troupe of actors who have been rehearsing a Broadway play has been murdered at the inn. To add to the stress, detective Harry Hunsacker (who Lt. Foster despises) and his assistant, Nigel Grouse are hired to investigate, the inn seems haunted, a mysterious stranger appears, and the body count just keeps on going up...

Period Music & Prizes for Guessing Who Done It

Vocalists, Patrick Detloff and Sarah Powell added an unexpected addition to the 1940's ambience by singing a selection of songs by Cole Porter and Ira Gershwin before the show and during the break. Audience members are also invited to predict who the killer/killers are by filling out ballots during intermission. The winner gets a prize at the end of the show.

Fun Photo Ops After the Show

Photography is not allowed during the performance but after the show, the actors are available for photos in the lobby. I was surprised at how well the Living Black and White™ make-up and costuming works offstage.

Plan your trip to the Pegasus Theatre's Living Black and White™ play
Website: pegasustheatre.org
Address: 2351 Performance Drive, Richardson, TX 75082

THURBER

Overview of Thurber, Texas

Thurber's heyday ran from the late 1880's through the 1930's when it was a major bituminous coal producer and the largest company town in Texas, with a population topping 10,000. Thurber also had the most prolific vitrified paving brick plant west of the Mississippi thanks to local clay deposits. These are the same red bricks you see in the Fort Worth Stockyards, the Galveston sea wall, Congress Avenue in Austin, Camp Bowie, and throughout many towns where the main roads are still paved with brick.

Thurber's 128-foot brick smokestack is what most people notice as they whiz by on their way to Abilene. It's all that remains of the power plant which, in 1895, made Thurber one of the very first electrified cities in the USA. By 1915, every home here was equipped with natural gas heating, another modern convenience provided by the company town.

Texas and Pacific Coal Company is "the company"to which I refer. It owned and operated everything in Thurber from the housing, restaurants, and stores, to the churches, cemetery, and opera house. The company even printed its own scrip, paper money that could be spent in the town of Thurber and nowhere else.

The local Catholic church was named St. Barbara after the patron saint of coal miners. The priest heard confession in several languages since Thurber's work force hailed from all over the world, including Italy, Poland, Ireland, and Russia.

A large percentage of Thurber residents were Italian, which may explain why the Metropolitan Opera troupe stopped there en-route from the east coast to the west coast. Thurber's opera house was pretty swanky for its day. Not only did it seat 665 patrons, but it included ceiling fans and private opera boxes.

The discovery of oil and the frenzy that ensued in its pursuit is what killed off Thurber. By 1935, most of its inhabitants had moved on to other livelihoods and the mines were abandoned. Texas and Pacific still owns the remaining 127 million tons of coal still buried beneath this once-thriving city.

Formerly the largest city between Fort Worth and El Paso, Thurber is now a ghost town. While the population has dwindled to five, don't let that fool you; this tiny burg offers a surprising amount of things to see, do, and even eat.

Smokestack Restaurant

Billed as "The Only Place to Eat in Downtown Thurber for Over 31 Years," the Smokestack Restaurant is pretty easy to find. As the name suggests, it is right beside the smokestack.

Open for breakfast, lunch, and dinner, the Bennett family and their crew serve up hearty meals made to order. The cuisine can best be described as good old southern comfort food and includes such items as chicken-fried steak, chicken-fried chicken, and grilled chicken livers. Sides include fried okra and sweet potato fries. For dessert, the buttermilk pie comes highly recommended. And yes, they offer free Wi-Fi.

Plan your trip to the Smokestack Restaurant
Website: smokestack.net
Address: 239 Private Road 741, Mingus, TX 76463

New York Hill

New York Hill is what locals called the fancy part of town, where the bigwigs who oversaw the company's operations lived. It's now home to a family-run restaurant and several historic buildings that have been restored and are open for tours, including a miner's home, a coal train car, a band stand, and St. Barbara church. The church is available for weddings and other special events.

New York Hill Restaurant

The Mills family opened New York Hill Restaurant in 1989 and, like the Smokestack Restaurant, it serves hearty southern food 7 days a week for breakfast, lunch and dinner and also offers free Wi-Fi. The eatery is housed in what was formerly Thurber's Episcopal church and dates from 1918. The walls are decorated with photos of old-town Thurber and the Mills family are happy to chat about the town's colorful history.

Plan your trip to the New York Hill Restaurant
Website: thurbernewyorkhill.com
Address: 292 County Road 107, Thurber, TX

W. K. Gordon Center for Industrial History of Texas

To learn more about the town of Thurber, coal mining, and what life was like in a company town, visit the W.K. Gordon Center Museum. Thurber's history includes riots, racism, greed, and battles for the rights of workers. To study the town of Thurber from boom to demise is to also learn about broader aspects of America's political, social, and cultural history from the late 1880's to the present.

Plan your trip to the W. K. Gordon Center
Website: http://www.tarleton.edu/gordoncenter/
Address: 65258 Interstate 20 (Take Exit 367), Mingus, Texas 76463

WAXAHACHIE

Overview of Waxahachie

Although the Texas State Legislature deemed Waxahachie the Crape Myrtle Capital of Texas, this charming town is also known as the Movie Capital of Texas (more than 30 have been filmed there) and the Gingerbread City (due to its abundance of ornately decorated Victorian homes.)

Waxahachie might have become the Nerd Capital of Texas as well, if construction plans for the world's biggest and most powerful particle accelerator had been carried out in the 1980's instead of being scrapped by the US Congress in 1993.

Waxahachie hosts several festivals throughout the year including the Scarborough Renaissance Festival in May, the Gingerbread Trail in June, the Crape Myrtle Festival in July, and a WWII Reenactment for Veteran's Day in November, among others.

No matter what is going on when you hit town, please note that while the origin of the name "Waxahachie" is up for debate, the pronunciation is not. The "wax" part of the word rhymes with "walks," not "whacks." Got it?

Movie Capital of Texas

In the 1980's, Hollywood discovered Waxahachie and used its historic buildings as the backdrop for several movies including three Academy Award winners, "Tender Mercies" (starring Robert Duvall), "The Trip to Bountiful" (starring Geraldine Page), and "Places in the Heart" (starring Sally Field, John Malkovich, and Danny Glover.) In addition, several episodes of the TV show "Walker, Texas Ranger" (starring Chuck Norris) were also filmed in Waxahachie.

Gingerbread City

One reason movies are shot in Waxahachie is because so many beautiful Victorian homes remain. The town's annual Gingerbread Trail allows visitors to tour several of them every June.

Crape Myrtle Capital of Texas

Often called "the lilac of the south," crape myrtles are hardy shrubs that bloom in a variety of bright colors ranging from white, to vivid shades of purple, pink, and red. Not only do crape myrtles thrive in Texas. They are among the longest-blooming shrubs, flowering for up to 4 months a year.

Every July, Waxahachie celebrates the official state shrub of Texas with its Crape Myrtle Festival, which includes parades, live music, fireworks, food stands, and more.

Ellis County Courthouse

At the heart of downtown, you will find a grand stone courthouse. If it strikes you as a super-sized version of the courthouse in Decatur, that's because both buildings were designed by James Riely Gordon in his Romanesque Revival style. The building is nine stories high, and includes both gray and pink granite, as well as red and cream colored sandstone.

Legend of Ellis County Courthouse

According to local lore, the stone faces adorning the Ellis County Courthouse reveal a tale of unrequited love. As the story goes, the man responsible for the courthouse carvings was in love with his landlord's daughter. At the start of their courtship, the craftsman carved beautiful, smiling faces. When she rebuffed his advances, his carvings reflected this rejection by becoming more and more macabre, with the last one depicting her as a grimacing ogre.

While that's a fun story, historians are quick to point out that the faces depicted on the courthouse are part of a centuries-old European design tradition, including characters such as the "Green Man," and other medieval caricatures of human emotions.

A lesser known tale regarding the Ellis County Courthouse, one that is actually true, is often referred to as the "dueling cornerstones." Instead of just one cornerstone, the Ellis County Courthouse has two. The first one shows the names of all the county commissioners involved in the initial vote to construct the courthouse. The second cornerstone displays the names of the commissioners who were in office when the construction was completed. Only one election separated these two occurrences, yet not a single name appears on both cornerstones. The explanation for this is a bit hazy, but the most widely accepted theory suggests that voters were so annoyed at the funds required for the courthouse that they voted all of them out of office.

Plan your trip to the Ellis County Courthouse
Address: 101 West Main St., Waxahachie, TX 75165

Scarborough Renaissance Festival

The Scarborough Renaissance Festival takes place on 35 acres of beautifully wooded land about a half hour's journey south of the Dallas – Fort Worth Metroplex on the outskirts of the town of Waxahachie.

This lively Texas Renaissance festival has been a regional favorite since it first opened in 1981. Each weekend from early April through the end of May, the grounds come to life with a cast of costumed characters who have fun reenacting life in medieval times – the year 1533, to be precise.

With over 200 "shoppes" and constant entertainment taking place on several stages, you may want to purchase a weekend pass. You simply cannot see it all in one day.

Anne Boleyn and Henry VIII hold court, lead medieval dances, parades, and occasionally mingle with common folk like you and me. Special events occur each weekend, such as caber tossing, falconry, jugglers, jousts and live music. While all the entertainers perform for free, many do pass a tip bucket at the end of their shows.

One of my favorites is the falconry demonstration, led by members of a non-profit wild bird rescue and rehabilitation center called Last Chance Forever. It's a wonderful opportunity to see hawks, owls, eagles and even a vulture up close.

There is plenty to learn from craftspeople who demonstrate the old ways at the Scarborough Renaissance Festival. As you wander through the village, you will see costumed artisans engaged in blacksmithing, glassblowing, candle-making, and more.

Photographs are encouraged, so shutterbugs need not be shy. Enter your best snaps in the Tournament of Images and you may even see yours in print. (See the official website for full contest rules and prize information.)

There are plenty of food choices for those with a hale and hearty appetite. Most items are more whimsical than historically accurate, such as, "steak on a stake," "fryed" macaroni, and the ever-popular turkey drumstick. Wash it all down with your choice of soft drinks or spirits, including a selection of ales, margaritas, or a potent honey mead.

It's certainly acceptable to wear shorts and a T-shirt; however, most attendees take the opportunity to dress up. No need to despair if your closet is lacking; there's a costume rental booth right by the entrance where you can find period garb at a reasonable price. Wooden wagons are also available in case your medieval crew includes a toddler or two.

So the next time you want to party like it's 1533, head on down to the Scarborough Renaissance Festival in Waxahachie, Texas. For more information, check out the official Scarborough Renaissance Festival website.

Plan your trip to the Scarborough Renaissance Festival
Website: srfestival.com
Address: 2511 Farm to Market 66, Waxahachie, TX 75167

Catfish Plantation

Dinner at the Catfish Plantation after spending a day at the Scarborough Renaissance Fair has become a tradition for my husband and me. The fact that we arrive in full ren-fair regalia is part of the fun.

The wait staff at the Catfish Plantation are friendly and the service is attentive, but slightly slower paced than some other places. We love it there.

As the name suggests, catfish is the house specialty. I also recommend the hush puppies, but try to leave room for dessert if you can.

The restaurant is located in a well-kept Victorian home built in 1895 surrounded by a big front yard and a white picket fence.

The residence is allegedly haunted, but don't be alarmed. All the ghosts are known to be friendly, although one is known for flirting with the ladies by playing with their long hair and tickling their knees. I've never had a paranormal encounter at the Catfish Plantation, but if it's slow enough to chat with the staff, they all have tales to tell.

The restaurant has been the subject of several paranormal investigations, and they never disappoint.

Plan your trip to the Catfish Plantation
Website: catfishplantation.com
Address: 814 Water Street, Waxahachie, TX 75165

Munster Mansion Replica

There is no official address for "1313 Mockingbird Lane" in Waxahachie, Texas. However, there is one fantastic looking replica of the Munster family home which Sandra and Charles McKee built in 2001 to depict the house from the classic TV sitcom.

Since it's a fictional house, the pair watched and re-watched all 70 episodes of the show to create their building plans. They even have a fire-breathing creature under the main staircase. Some rooms, such as the bathroom, were never shown in the series, so they were able to wing it in those sections.

Who are the Munsters?

For those who don't know, "The Munsters" is an American TV sitcom from the mid-1960's with a really catchy theme song. The show followed the antics of a quirky-but-harmless monster family. While the father was

Frankenstein-esque, the grandfather, the mother and the son were all vampiric in looks. This, in contrast, made the pretty blond daughter into the family misfit. (I really can't do it justice here, so for more about the TV show, check out the official Munster Mansion website)

Annual Munster Mansion Halloween Charity Open House

While Sandra and Charles McKee have clearly put a lot of effort into their Munster Mansion recreation, it is not meant to be a year-round tourist attraction or museum. For them, it is simply a fun project. Even so, since 2002, Sandra and Charles McKee have sponsored a 2-day Munster Mansion Open House in October with all proceeds going to local charities, such as the Ellis County SPCA and the Salvation Army. A shuttle bus is used to ferry visitors back and forth, since the Munster Mansion is out in the country.

Besides all the hard work the couple puts into setting up this open house, the McKee's always try to have at least one actor from the original show attend the party. In 2012, Butch Patrick (who played Eddie Munster) showed up to greet the crowd, and tour the mansion. In 2013, Pat Priest (who played Marilyn Munster) pulled up in a limousine, signed autographs, and chatted with fans.

For more information, such as the exact dates of this year's Munster Mansion Halloween Open House, as well as an excellent video interview with the Sandra and Charles McKee check out the official Munster Mansion website.

Plan your trip to the Munster Mansion

Website: munstermansion.com

WEATHERFORD

Overview of Weatherford

Weatherford is the county seat for Parker County and is known as the "Cutting Horse Capital of the World." In case you're wondering, a cutting horse is one that has been trained to single out a specific cow from the rest of the herd - an important skill for cowboys driving cattle to market. While the Chisolm Trail is no longer used to drive cattle overland, the sport of training cutting horses is alive and well in Weatherford, where competitions are held throughout the year. Many famous horse trainers live here.

The Texas State legislature also named Weatherford the "Peach Capital of Texas." Even though the city's annual peach festival is only one day long, it attracts over 45,000 visitors each summer.

Plan your trip to the Parker Country Peach Festival
Website: parkercountypeachfestival.org

Parker County Courthouse

The ornate brick building in the middle of Weatherford's town square is the fourth building to stand in that same spot. The first three were destroyed by suspected arson, although no one was ever charged for those crimes. The present courthouse was erected in 1886 and cost $55,555.55 to build. That must be Weatherford's lucky number, because unlike its predecessors, this one has yet to burst into flames.

Plan your trip to the Parker County Courthouse
Address: 123 N Main St, Weatherford, TX

Peter Pan a.k.a. Mary Martin statue

Mary Martin, the performer most strongly identified with role of Peter Pan, was born in Weatherford, Texas. This talented singer and actress was also the first to play Maria von Trapp in The Sound of Music, as well as Nellie Forbush in South Pacific.

In 1976, artist Ronald Thomason created a life-sized bronze of Mary Martin as Peter Pan. The sculpture still stands in front of the Weatherford Public Library.

I must also say that while the sculpture is good, it doesn't quite convey how beautiful Mary Martin is. Check out some photos of her online and you will see what I mean.

I found it interesting to learn that Larry Hagman was Mary Martin's son. He, too, became a famous actor, known especially for his roles on television as the astronaut Major Anthony Nelson in the 1960's comedy "I Dream of Jeannie" and J.R. Ewing in the 1980's nighttime soap opera "Dallas."

Doss Heritage & Culture Center

To find out more about Mary Martin, Larry Hagman, and more Weatherford lore, spend an afternoon at the Doss Heritage and Culture Center. What started as a local library exhibit has expanded into a full museum that's well worth visiting. Fans of Larry McMurtry's book *Lonesome Dove* (and, hey, if you call yourself Texan this ought to be you!) will enjoy the Trail Drivers exhibit which focuses on Charles Goodnight and Oliver Loving, the cattlemen who inspired Larry McMurtry's novel.

Plan your trip to the Doss Heritage and Culture Center
Website: dosscenter.org
Address: 1400 Texas Dr, Weatherford, TX 76086

The First Monday Trade Days

Despite what the name implies, the First Monday Trade Days is NOT held on the first Monday of the month. Weatherford's First Monday Trade Days is open to the public from 9:00 a.m. - 4:00 p.m. on the Friday, Saturday and Sunday before the first Monday of each month. Trust me, if you show up on Monday as I did, there will be nothing going on.

Once you've gotten that confusion out of the way, this monthly open air market is well worth checking out. Weatherford's First Monday Trade Days is one of the oldest outdoor markets in Texas. It began in the mid-1800's when the Parker County Courthouse held legal trials at the beginning of each month. These proceedings attracted vendors, who would stand in the shade of the courthouse to sell their wares. This soon became a large open-air market, with ranchers, homesteaders, and other vendors buying, selling, and trading amongst each other. The tradition continued into the new millennium, and Weatherford's First Monday Trade Days still offers a wide variety of goods, including livestock and farm fresh produce.

Plan your trip to First Monday Trade Days

Website: ci.weatherford.tx.us
Address: Santa Fe and Hwy 180, Weatherford, Texas 76086

Chandor Gardens

Twenty-five miles west of Fort Worth lies a beautifully landscaped garden in the Historic District of

Weatherford, Texas. This lush oasis was created by the internationally renowned portrait artist, Douglas Chandor, and his wife, Ina. Chandor Gardens is such an unspoiled treasure, part of me selfishly wanted to keep it as my own little secret garden rather than include it in this book.

At a mere 4 acres, Chandor Gardens can hardly compete with the likes of the 66-acre Dallas Arboretum or the 109-acre Fort Worth Botanic Gardens, but this is part of its charm. After all, even in Texas, bigger isn't always better.

It's so well-planned that each little section of the garden offers visitors a surprising amount of privacy. There are plenty of nooks and crannies perfect for stealing a kiss from your sweetheart as you wander along the pathways.

Chandor Gardens as Living Art

Douglas Chandor called these gardens a form of "living art." It really does feel like you are walking through a painting in places. The landscaping is a mixture of traditional English style gardens, with Asian influences. Some of my favorite features include the koi pond, the 30-foot waterfall and the bronze sea dragon fountain.

Douglas Chandor was born in Surrey, England in 1897. He began his career as a soldier, however, not an artist. In 1918, while recovering from illness and injuries sustained during WWI, Chandor rediscovered his childhood love of painting.

He must have been a quick study, because within a year, Chandor began receiving prestigious portrait commissions. One thing led to another, and in 1921 he completed a portrait of the Prince of Wales which officially launched his career.

Soon after, Chandor was commissioned to paint President Herbert Hoover, the Vice President Charles Curtis, and the entire White House cabinet. His portrait career was extremely successful and included such notable figures as Queen Elizabeth II, President Franklin Roosevelt, Joseph Stalin, and Prime Minister Winston Churchill (who was quite an artist in his own right.) You can see some of Douglas Chandor's paintings (as well as some of Winston Churchill's watercolors) at the Dallas Museum of Art.

Why Weatherford, Texas?

If Chandor was British, how the heck did he wind up in Weatherford, Texas? Just like me, he landed in the Lone Star State because he fell in love with a Texan. In Chandor's case, he divorced his first wife in 1932. Two years later, he married Ina Kuteman Hill. I'm not sure where the pair met, but Ms. Hill hailed from Weatherford, which is why the couple opted to spend half of the year in her family's north Texas mansion and the other half in New York City.

White Shadows Garden

Soon after marrying, Douglas and Ina Chandor began an ambitious landscaping project they called, "White Shadows Garden." From 1936 until 1952, the pair transformed the barren yard of their estate into intricate gardens.

After Mr. Chandor's death in 1953, his widow renamed the place "Chandor Gardens" in his honor and opened them to the public to defray the cost of upkeep.

Paradise Lost – Almost!

This arrangement worked well enough until Ina Chandor's death in 1978. With no heirs to maintain their project, the once magnificent gardens slowly deteriorated and the estate sat empty.

Fortunately, in 1995 Charles and Melody Bradford bought the site and began the slow, steady process of restoring the site to its former glory. In 2002, the city of Weatherford purchased Chandor Gardens from the Bradfords and opened it to the public once again.

Weddings, Garden Parties & Tours

Chandor Gardens is available for weddings and garden parties. People can rent the garden, the mansion, or both for private functions. Imagine what a whimsical garden party you could host there.

Plan your trip to Chandor Gardens
Website: chandorgardens.mynewsarchive.com
Address: 711 W. Lee Avenue, Weatherford TX 76086

WICHITA FALLS

The Falls at Lucy Park

Despite the name Wichita Falls, after the original waterfall was destroyed by a flood in 1886, it wasn't until 1987 that a 54-foot man-made waterfall was created for the public to enjoy.

The waterfalls can be seen by southbound traffic on I-44, and are well worth checking out. From what I've read elsewhere, the falls can be muddy after heavy rains, and at other times are only a mere trickle. When I visited, however, the water was flowing in full force, and they were a pretty sight.

Even if the waterfalls aren't flowing when you visit, Lucy Park is a nice place to stretch your legs, since it is well-landscaped and its paths are smoothly paved. I'm not sure if it was just our GPS, but even though we could see the falls from the highway, it took us a few tries to actually figure out where to park and how to access them.

Plan your trip to The Falls in Lucy Park
Website: wichitafallstx.gov

Address: 100 Sunset Dr, Wichita Falls, TX 76302

The World's Smallest Skyscraper

Built in 1919, the Newby-McMahon Building in downtown Wichita Falls is more commonly referred to as "the world's smallest skyscraper."

J.D. McMahon was an engineer and oilman from Philadelphia. He proposed adding a high-rise section to the original building to that it could house more office space.

McMahon quickly raised $200,000 (a fortune for that time) to construct an office building according to plans he drew up. At a glance, it appeared that the finished building would stand 48 stories high, and McMahon never said otherwise. Unfortunately for the investors, no one noticed the teeny little decimal points in the blueprints; this meant the building would actually stand 480 inches tall, not 480 feet, as everyone assumed.

McMahon constructed the building using his own crew, and it didn't take long for investors to realize they had been conned. When they attempted to sue McMahon, however, the judge threw the case out because McMahon had followed to the letter the plans the investors had signed off on. In the end, McMahon split town with a big chunk of cash before construction was completed, and the city was left with an embarrassing reminder of the importance of reading the fine print.

This odd little building is still standing and has been designated a Texas Historic Landmark. When I visited, it was undergoing renovation and was not open for touring. Even so, it is worth driving by if you happen to be in town.

Plan your trip to the World's Smallest Skyscraper
Address: 701 La Salle, Wichita Falls, TX

References:

Texas State Historical Association: *A Digital Gateway to Texas History*, website: **http://www.tshaonline.org/**

Jennifer Ramsey, (2005), *A Lady's Day Out in Dallas and Surrounding Areas Vol. II*, A Lady's Day Out, Fort Worth, TX

Amy K. Brown, (2008), *Backroads & Byways of Texas*, The Countryman Press, Woodstock, VT

Kay McCasland Threadgill, (2005), *Exploring Dallas with Children*, A Republic of Texas Press Book, Taylor Trade Publishing, an imprint of The Rowman & Littlefield Publishing Group, Inc., Lanham, MD

John A. Haslet, (1984), *Famous Trees of Texas*, Texas Forest Service: A Part of the Texas A&M University System, TX

Bob Phillips, (1993), *52 Offbeat Texas Stops*, Phillips Productions, Inc., Dallas, TX

Kinky Friedman, (2003), *Kinky Friedman's Guide to Texas Etiquette*, Perennial, an imprint of HarperCollins, New York, NY

Jerome Pohlen, (2006*), Oddball Texas: A Guide to Some Really Strange Places*, Chicago Review Press, Chicago, IL

Carrie Shook and Robert L. Shook, (1990), *Only in Texas*, Perigee Books, an imprint of The Putnam Publishing Group, New York, NY

Laura Trim, (1985), *Short Trips In and Around Dallas*, LDT Press, Dallas, TX

Andy Rhodes, (2009), *Moon Texas (Moon Handbooks)*, Moon Publications, Inc., Chico, CA

James E. Gaskin, (2011), *Texas Hysterical Society: The Wacky Side of the Lone Star State*, Atriad Press, Mesquite, TX

Sharry Buckner, (2009), *Texas Little Trips: Great Getaways Near You*, Atriad Press, Dallas, TX

June Naylor, (2002), *Texas Off the Beaten Path: A Guide to Unique Places*, The Globe Pequot Press, Guilford, CT

John Kelso, updated and revised by Sharry Buckner, (2011), *Texas Curiosities: Quirky Characters, roadside oddities & other offbeat stuff*, The Globe Pequot Press, Guilford, CT

June Naylor, (2005), *Quick Escapes: Dallas - Fort Worth*, The Globe Pequot Press, Guilford, CT

Acknowledgments:

Whether you hired me to write for you, helped me with technical problems, played Words with Friends with me in the middle of the night, or simply offered a kind word at the right time, I couldn't have completed this book without the kindness, encouragement, and assistance I received from the following:

Woofmutt, Owain Thomas, Cherrye Moore, Mary Jo Manzanares, Morgan Dragonwillow, Nicole Rivera, Patricia Lynne, Brett Jonas, The StoryDam Twitter chat peeps, Andrew Crusoe, DFWcon, Arlee Bird & all the A to Z Blog Challenge peeps, Joy Daley, Paul Acciavatti, Michelle Fabio, Michelle Perlmutter, David Sumoflam Kravetz, Paula Puffer, Andy & Ann Butchard, Gilbert Malone, Naomi Morlan, Karma Tenzing Wangchuk, Doug Faber, Dan & Jan Stober, John Fahrenwald, Andrew Hoenninger, Lou Antonelli, Mike Gilmore, Laree Griffith, Ray Huyghe, , Angelo Petrelli, Allen Payne, Kalliope ...

...and every single person who ever commented on my blog!

Made in the USA
Middletown, DE
09 June 2015